SABOTAGE

How to Stop Killing Your Relationship Because Of
Commitment Phobias

I Love You Too Death

Johanna Sparrow

DEDICATION

I dedicate this book to all of my loyal readers. Thank you for all of your support, may this book bless each and every one who reads it.

CONTENTS

Johanna Sparrow

ACKNOWLEDGMENTS

I would like to acknowledge Terry Lou for his great editing work on helping me get this book out. I also would like to thank the cover designer, Sanja StojKovic for such a great cover!

`

Foreword

How many people do you know that have been in relationships that have left them devastated because of commitment phobes? The truth is, I know many people who have gone through this and have become fearful of dating. I like to call this the love'em and leave'em, phase of finding Mr. or Mrs. Right. How many of you are dating someone today who just won't commit to you? You question yourself as if it's your fault for the many damaged relationships you've had over the years. What you need to know is that the ending of a relationship with a commitment phobe who won't commit to you is never your fault.

Why are you constantly meeting commitment phobes? Dating and falling in love with a commitment phobe can leave you angry and confused. Most people who are in this type of dating cycle have no clue what's going on around them. Is this to say commitment phobes are bad people, no they just have a hard time loving someone. Loving or being in a relationship with a commitment phobe can make for a very stressful relationship. If you don't want to live your relationship in a dark room you have to open your eyes to the person you are trying to have a future with. This is not to say that a commitment phobe will never get married because many of them do, but they make their marriage a living hell. Being married to a commitment phobe does not stop the commitment phobe from their fears once in a relationship. Many people who are in relationships with commitment phobes are full of pain and hurt. It's no fun living in a nightmare where you end up loving someone more than they love you. A commitment phobe knows just what to say to you to get what they want, as well as how to say it to make you weak in the knees. They always seem to touch your heart by saying the right words at the right moment, you find yourself caught in their life stories, saddened over their heartbreaks. They can sell you anything which makes them the perfect salesperson. They would tell you that no one understands them more than you and you believe them. You end up loving the funny, witty and sassy sense of humor they project.

Many commitment phobes are secretive when it comes to their personal life yet they don't mind telling you their life stories because they are covered in lies mainly to win you over. If you have ever been in a relationship with a commitment phobe you known nothing is off limits, you talk about everything and seem to have more things in common then you expected. A commitment phobe has had many of the same dating horrors as you but seems to add more details to pull on your heart strings. In the beginning of getting to know a commitment phobe you find yourself amazed by their words, ways, caring and open spirit. Sure you want to tell the world about this new person you've just met but it is too soon, so you question whether they are real or not.

If you really want to know what type of person you are really dating just ask those closest to you, they can spot a commitment phobe in seconds, they have no problem letting you know what's up. Family and friends are not taken by a commitment phobes's sweet words and phony behaviors. I am sure your family members are the last people on earth that you would want to know your business especially if you feel you have met someone special. This is not to say that you are not able to see what's going on, you are just not ready to see what issues may be lurking around since all you can see is one amazing, loving, caring, respectful and trustworthy person. By the time you see what everyone around you is talking about it's too late, your heart is involved. You are noticing things about this person you've never noticed before since the relationship is moving in another direction and they seem unsure if they are on board. The worse part about being in a relationships with a commitment phobe is that you do not get feedback when addressing their behavior, leaving you confused.

It's never easy dealing with a commitment phobe in a relationship since you will never have the true relationship that you are looking for as long as you are dating them. Oh, how I wish people had descriptions of what they are like in relationships stamped on their forehead, dating would be easier. Commitment phobes love to lie you could find yourself falling apart as you search for the truth once involved with them. Once you've experienced a commitment phobe you will never be the same, you will never let anyone lie, hurt or cause you pain again. Dating is never easy because you have to trust someone you don't know anything about which can be pretty scary if you've been hurt a few times. Finally I will show you what to look for when it comes to dating a commitment phobe so you can conquer this beast of being a victim in relationships.

My intention is to teach you how to detect and understand the behavior of the commitment phobe so you come out a winner in love.

Introduction

My experiences in dealing with commitment phobes who will never commit no matter how hard they try to convenience you is what has brought me to this topic. Finding the right person who understands you and vibes with you like no other is what you are looking for, trust me I know. I am sure this is what you are looking for but somehow, you keep attracting the commitment phobe. What signals are you sending that catches the commitment phobe's eye? If you have found yourself once again in another relationship with someone who was very convincing in wanting a relationship only to see those same behaviors of commitment issues rear its ugly head you must check yourself to see if you are radiating something they want. Face it sometimes we want love and we want it so fast that we settle for someone that looked our way once or twice. Some people jump into relationships like changing underwear not knowing what they are getting. Are you more in love with the idea of being in love instead of finding the right person that can love you? What makes dating a commitment phobe someone you should avoid dating all together? What's the big rush on love? Take your time when it comes to dating someone so that you are not filled with regrets later on. Love should never lie, cause pain, hurt or humiliate you ever. If you are not looking for a commitment or to settle down then I still say approach dating with caution since you may be dating a commitment phobe. I have friends who fell in love with commitment phobes when falling in love was the last thing on their minds. Their pain and hurt was real, they found it hard to get out of a relationship they never wanted so one can imagine what they would have went through if they were looking for love only to have their heart taken by a commitment phobe.

Commitment phobes have no problem faking their feelings to get you to give them your heart. Their behaviors and actions are damaging and dangerous when it comes to being in a relationship. Your relationship with a commitment phobe is doomed from the start which you won't know until the last minute or when they are on their way out the door. Commitment phobes have no problem breaking hearts or causing chaos in your life. If you have get a chance to see past the charade, you will never forget them and will never let it happen again. Let's face it we've all been hurt in relationships where we have gotten past it, not the same for a commitment phobe. Their fears of being hurt or being left keeps them from giving you the one thing that you want, their heart. Than you have the functioning commitment phobe who has mastered going that extra mile by staying in a long term relationship or marrying. These charades are in place to make you believe in them and nothing else, they are still afraid of love and commitment. Long time relationships and marriages with commitment phobes are plagued with more problems than other relationships due to fears, hurts and pains clouding/affecting the commitment phobe's judgment to let you in. I am sure you know how to date and what to look for when it comes to the type of person you want to commit to. Do you know what to look for when it comes to dealing with a commitment phobe? Are you aware that as you go out meeting people to be a part of your life a commitment phobe is also looking for someone they can trick and lie too.

I am sure in your past relationships there were a lot of signs you missed or overlooked for the sake of the relationship. Did they pick arguments to get out of committing to you? Did you stay confused a lot in your past relationships? Were your words twisted in past relationships to make you look like the villain? Were you catching them in lies every time they opened their mouth? Were your arguments about your relationships with family or friends causing you to abandon your friends and family in order for your relationship to work? These are just some of the red flags a commitment phobe will throw into a relationship blindsiding your efforts at happiness. A commitment phobe is a straight forward manipulator when it comes to relationships, they use your desire to settle down as a weapon to control you. I've had friends as well as myself experience these things before finding my soul mate and I tell you I was so confused by what was going on I had to take a break from dating, I did not blame myself for what was happening like many do. It's no fun being fooled by someone whose looking to hurt you by not getting hurt.

A commitment phobe has a certain way about themselves that make you feel like they are too good to be true, it's true! Having a son and daughter in the dating world, one of my biggest fears is them meeting up with a commitment phobe. My husband and I have prepared them to know the signs of these types of people right away

When you find yourself connecting lies like dots on a puzzle in your relationship, that's when you know it's over. The person you thought was the one for you, is not what or who they claimed to be, you gave a lot of yourself to them while they played with your emotions. You're hurt and angry but just know it's not the end of the world, you will find that special person when you least expect it. You need to learn who and what you can and can't date in order to be happy, no matter how good the person looks or how nice they are to you. You are fooling yourself if you've convinced yourself that because of past relationships you are becoming a commitment phobe. Anyone can be a commitment phobe but, if you are still desiring to be in a committed relationship you are far from becoming a commitment phobe. Many commitment phobes are unable to commit or be faithful in their relationships. Stop believing that every person you meet or asks you out is safe to date until you really get to know them.

I want for you to walk away with the understanding that your goals and dreams are personal until you are ready to share them, anybody who is interviewing you for that information on a date has other plans in mind. Know that you are not the first person to have fallen for someone that is smooth and you will not be the last. You will however stop being the one getting hurt over love by knowing what to look for. But how can you tell if you are dealing with a commitment phobe? Keep reading and you will know the signs and behaviors of some of the best imitators of love. If you are really ready to learn the truth about commitment phobes and how they operate when it comes making you fall in love with them, keep reading and I will see you on the next page!

CHAPTER 1
ARE YOU THE ONE?

How many times have you heard someone tell you that you are the one they have been looking for all of their life? I am sure it's been said to you a thousand times. I take it, we've all heard this said to us at one time or another. But what does it really mean? Many of my friends and family members have been down this road including myself before getting married, I caution you to keep your eyes and ears open for people like this in the dating world. You will be able to smell a rat as soon as they start becoming everything you need. We all want to find that special person to share our lives with one day.

Don't be fooled by someone telling you that you are the one. Strong relationships are built on love, respect, trust and honesty. The key is finding someone shares the same interest as you and wants the same things in life as you. Let's say you are at the store and come face to face with the man woman of your dreams.

You muster up the courage to say something followed by exchanging your numbers and your first date is tonight because you are just that eager to see them again. Make sure you pay attention to everything that's said to you on the first date since the person will paint themselves in a good light. Don't think for one second everything that's being told to you is the truth, take some things with a grain of salt until proven otherwise.

If you are the honest type know that not everyone will be like you on the first date. People have motives when it comes to dating, it's your job to know what their motives are. I am not telling you to walk around paranoid when it comes to dating, just be careful.

Are you a hopeless romantic? Then you may be looking to fall in love at first sight. Love at first sight can mean a host of things, one being that the person is different from you but you can find that you have some things in common like their style of dress. When you get around to that first date make sure you are not the only one talking. This is important since very few people know that talking too much and telling too much about yourself allows a commitment phobe to know their next move.

A commitment phobes job is to study you so later they can impress you. You are allowing yourself to be studied when you are out on a date for the first time when you can't stop talking. How important is it to tell your date how much you love video games or that you just purchased several SCI Fi Cd's, it's not important but what you did give away was your spending habits, I am sure they will be looking for some nice gifts later on. The more you share about the things you love, the more they will use them to win you over. This is how so many people become victims of sabotage in relationships by a commitment phobe.

The one thing I have learned in my study of commitment phobes is that they do not trust anyone. The information you feed them gives them the confidence needed to win you over. Outside of you not telling them anything they are at a loss for words. Sure you are thinking this is not my situation but ask yourself if you were the one who did most of the talking on the first date? If your answer is yes then I am sure you have given away more than you know.

It does not matter if it's the first date or the fourth date. A person with commitment issues listens for those key words within the conversation to help guide them in getting what they want from you quickly, then they are out the door. Did you know that many people walking around today in relationships struggle with relationship issues. This is not just a dating problem, no sir! If you are the type of person who loves to share how loyal and trusting you would be in a relationship, a commitment phobe will love you. They have nothing to worry about since you will drive the relationship while they lie their way into your heart.

A commitment phobe learns to play off of your issues and emotions as if it's a compass guiding them to your heart. They know what to say, as well as how to say it. They make you laugh at the right time and right moment. They are sweet, keeping you at a loss for words. At times you believe it's too good to be true because of how well they know you. Is it safe to say that because of how this person makes you feel that you have become caught up in the moment of love, not seeing anything else? Don't allow yourself to be blinded by their dating performances, you need to snap out of it to look around for the truth which I am sure is staring you right in the face. How did this person take your heart so quickly? How do they know so much about you? I am sure you feel that you both are alike but the truth is you gave them way too much information on your first few dates.

It's not easy identifying someone with commitment issues unless you know exactly what to look for. For many people identifying a person with commitment issues can be difficult to spot since they play off of your mood, emotions and needs. This does not mean that your relationship with such a person is not real you just have to look for patterns and know what questions to ask. Love can sweep you off of your feet in the matter of seconds, so can a commitment phobe. It's your job to see the real person from the fraud. If you don't question why things are going so fast you will continue to fall, missing out on the truth.

When most people say that love is blind they are not talking about being taken advantage of by someone pretending to love them. Yes, love and the feeling of being in love is an amazing thing if you keep your eyes open to the truth and clearly listen to what is being said to you.

I remember talking to an old friend of mine named April who fell in love with some guy she met on a dating site. Half way into hearing all about their relationship. she mentioned how he told her that he, lust her before hanging up the phone, he would text it to her as well. Shocked by what I heard and not sure if she was aware of what she said, I asked her to repeat it. Her exact words, "He tells me that he, lust me every night before ending our call." Was it me or did she not hear what was being said to her? I heard it loud and clear, lust not love which means their relationship was all about sex. April was so caught up in all the sweet things this guy was saying that she failed to hear what his true intentions were.

This is similar to how someone with commitment issues will cause you to lose focus by impressing you with what you want to hear, in April's case she wanted to be desired which she clearly got. Now that I have gotten your attention, are you ready learn the behaviors of a commitment phobe? You don't have to have a broken heart to understand the cruelty of some people's intentions. Don't be afraid to date someone who is saying all of the right things just use common sense, never take it at face value. Pay attention to their behavior when they think you are not watching them.

Know that their friends can be a good resource of information so get to know them. Always listen to what they are saying, do not question them but find out what you need to know from their family and friends. If you are still not sure if the person you are dating has commitment phobias just keep turning the page, I am sure you will know by the time you finish this book. What are some of the signs that say you are being deceived by a commitment phobe?

- A commitment phobe is always in the rush to get you to believe them.
- A commitment phobe wants you to show them the same affection in return.
- A commitment phobe promises you everything, but delivers nothing.
- A commitment phobe builds you up one day only to tear you down days later.
- A commitment phobe wants you to express to them that you believe they are the one but becomes upset when you do not believe them.
- A commitment phobe acts nice and sweet for a moment, once you have brought into the lies, they are cruel and inconsiderate with your feelings.
- A commitment phobe wants you to feel taken care of by them, they know what you need and want. They have no problem with expressing that, but keep listening and looking because it will not last long.

Besides saying all of the right things and having the right things in common a commitment phobe is not interested in building a foundational relationship with you because they live life in the fast lane which allows them to get in and out of relationships very quickly.

At first glance a commitment phobe can be a real catch, but that's if you are not looking for anything in terms of a long lasting committed relationship. Anything more than a few weeks or months of dating you can kiss your heart goodbye. What makes dating or even marrying a commitment phobe so bad is that they never mean with they say, life is a game to them along with your feelings. They are not looking for those individuals who want short term relationships with no commitment, they are looking for individuals who want more, even marriage, that's where they become dangerous.

Loving a commitment phobe is like drinking poison, depending on what type of poison you are drinking, you may drop dead right away, but I am sure your heart will suffer long before you drop dead. Let's just say, the grim reaper of death is similar to the commitment phobe of relationships. If you're involved with them, your heart will suffer or stop beating when you find out they will never commit to you now that you have invested so much into them. This is one ride you should not take once you see the truth about a commitment phobe. Their love is deadly!

What was Their Longest Relationship?

Now that you have gotten yourself together for this date your thoughts are like many you've had which is, you plan to be bored to death or impressed out of your mind which is not what turns you on to liking someone. Sadly, this date will be like nothing you've ever experienced?

At this stage it does not matter where or how, you both met. What does matter is that your conversation may have been brief but you wanted to talk more. I have been told by many I know that it was the mysterious feel they got from the person that kept them wanting to know more about their life ultimately entrapping them in a web of lies. Sure you are thinking that's not going to happen to you since you are fully aware of what's going on. The truth is you don't know what will happen, you only know what that person allows you to know which is important in knowing the truth about someone early on.

Since going out you are amazed by everything this person says to you, it feels like an outer body experience. In your effort to really get to know them you make sure you plan the date where you can go somewhere quiet to just talk. In the beginning of a new relationship you find yourself sharing more than the other person, you love how they are engaged in every story you tell them. Finally you get to the questions about relationships from how long yours lasted to the terrible things the person did to you. You are comforted with smiles, shocked by the person's responses to your stories, finally they ask that question we all have asked on a date. What are you looking for? This is where you really want to tread lightly since you don't want to give too much away and sound like a puppy in need of a home.

Instead you dive right in with your heart and feelings to find that what you are saying is inciting a positive response on that person's face that cannot be hidden. Although you hear a small voice inside telling you to stop talking you ignore it since you feel you both are in a good place. What you fail to realize at this time is they are learning more about you, while you are learning less about them. Now if you can only keep your mouth closed long enough to see it.

By the time your realize it they know about you, your job, family, past relationships, and your first grade teacher, Ms. Rose, damn! Are you talking this much out of nerves or comfort? In any case it needs to stop now. By the time they tell you their story it's short and sweet or long and sad, either way you will feel a variety of emotions. Your facial expression will tell them all they need to know, hook line and sinker. From there, they keep you guessing playing on your heart strings as if you were a human violin.

I can tell you are probably thinking how sad, I would never do that to you if you were my_____. Go ahead, put your name on the line.

When looking for someone with commitment phobias you really don't have far to look. Below are five keys used by commitment phobes you must be aware of.

- o The commitment phobe is either quiet or overly confident.
- o The commitment phobe loves hearing you talk in the beginning than later tells you that you talk too much.
- o The commitment phobe loves to ask more questions on the first few dates as a way to get to know you, but they give very little information about themselves. *Secretive!*
- o The commitment phobe is always aiming to please even if you are not looking for anything.
- o The commitment phobe always tends to have had the same experiences you've had when it comes to relationships, they are quick to tell you so that you feel a connection. *The set up!*

If you want to keep a level head about everything that's happening to you right now, I say date with your eyes and ears open. Sure your ears can be open if your eyes are not !It's call using your blind sense. Don't be the first one to give so much away in the first stage of getting to know someone. The less someone knows about you the more you know about them. Now that you've got this section down pat let's keep moving.

Do They Sound Like a Poet?

Follow me for a minute as I take you on what a commitment phobe poet sounds like. Maybe you know what they sound like or just don't have a clue. Anyway, I am happy to show you the difference in a poet and the poet with issues. How many times have you met a person whose words flow out of their mouth like a song? No, I am not talking about someone who writes poetry but rather someone who knows what to say to make you feel good. In fact, this person has studied what you want, to the extent that you both feel an unbreakable bond.

Don't kid yourself, this is not a real poet but to you their words are magical. Who is this wonderful human being that's crossed your path? You must feel like the luckiest person in the world to have met someone so unique. At the end of the day don't flatter yourself this is one of the MOs the commitment phobe uses, wink!

The danger of the commitment phobe lover is that once they get you caught up in their world along with the things they say, they are no longer interested. The game is over, but they have to keep you wanting more, so in their bag of tricks they go where they offer you than just the poetic side of themselves. *Sounds sexy, right*!

If you are dating someone like this, know that in the beginning they will sweep you off your feet with kind, inspirational words that ring your way. I've learned that people with commitment phobias will not give up after the first trick in the bag is out, they have many more where that came from to woo you into falling harder than you've ever fallen for anyone. *Gotcha!*

Did you not notice that when you told this person that you loved their poetic side they seemed to say more? Oh! Yes, the commitment phobe loves attention. Did you also notice the more you blushed when the poetry was about you they smiled and laughed? If you paid attention when they laughed you would have noticed that smile on their face was one that clearly said, oh baby I gotcha! From here it's going to only get worse. Someone who is a commitment phobe is not looking to stay longer than they have to, it does not matter how happy you two seem, they will not stick around.

Day after day you see more of their talents and enjoy how they keep a smile on your face. The commitment phobe's goal is to make you fall in love with lies. But if you really think about it, you know nothing about this person other than them trying to win you over, period. And your insecure butt, loves it!

If you are like me then I am sure that you have seen lots of relationships like this, you may have also been in your fair share of relationships where that person impressed you so much that everything they said was like poetry, until you got to know the real person they had hiding inside. *And you were ghost!*

Below are a list of a few lines or sayings one may use in order to win over your heart with lies.

- o A commitment phobe loves giving you a pet name before there is a clear understanding to where the relationship is heading. Baby, sweetie, boo, lover, beautiful, handsome, sexy eyes, etc. you get the picture!
- o A commitment phobe loves sending you poetry they've found on the internet or in a book, they than claim to have written it just for you. Titles such as, I am thinking of you. *Rolling my eyes!*
- o Commitment phobe loves to send links to songs that express how they are feeling at the time which are usually songs about falling in love or you being the one. Those feelings are based on lies.
- o A commitment phobe will text you throughout the day with symbols and words like hugs, kisses and miss you. *Rolling eyes to the back of my head!*

Whenever you talk on the phone with a commitment phobe they will always want you to know that they have been thinking about you all day and was just about to call. This one is big because this is where they try to tie in how strong of a connection you have with each other since you beat them to the call first. *Holding my head!*

To take it one step further a commitment phobe will have no problems with posting enduring, expressive poems about their feelings for you on any social media knowing it's a bunch of lies.

Sure you have seen this type of person before because your sister, friend or brother dated them. Maybe you have never met anyone like this and their behavior is mind blowing. Nevertheless don't be fooled by this in the beginning because in time it will surely change.

I know you are thinking, this is the best person you have met so far in your life and you two get along well, so why in the hell would Johanna take them away from me? I hope you can see and hear the bullshit that's flowing your way. My advice is don't be fooled by what you hear because it can take your mind off of what you really need to focus on. What can you do to not be caught off guard by the niceness of someone you are getting to know until they can prove that they are genuine? Below are a list of do's and don'ts you need to know during the get to know the poet phase of dating?

- o Do listen clearly to what is being said to you and how, so that you don't take things the wrong way.
- o Don't lose yourself over highly expressive or enduring post on social media or sent to you in text. The person still has to prove themselves to be genuine.
- o Pay attention to everything that is said to you in the early stages of your relationship because you will need that information as a reference when things change.
- o Don't pour out your life story or those that you love to the person in the early stages of your relationship. You may seem like you are being forth coming about truths and hurt in your life, but it ends up being the stock pile of ammunition used against you later on?
- o Say thank you even if you think it's too soon for so much emotion and lovely words of endearment. You can still take it all in without it going to your head while still being on guard.
- o Never give too much away in the terms of how you are feeling. You don't want to be shot down with that information later on by that commitment phobe you are dating.

Love and expressing one's feeling can be a wonderful thing but many times we rush in without thinking, ending up torn to shreds because of our need for love and relationship that can take over our ability to see, listen and feel what's going on around us. Building up to these things should be the steps you are looking for. If that person feels they need to express their heart to you, let them but make sure your disclaimer is out for them to read. Your disclaimer when it comes to being in a new relationship should be to look, listen and feel nothing else. Do not give too much away, I cannot express that enough. When dealing with a commitment phobe being able to see, in addition to hearing what is going on, is the key to not ending up disappointed?

Are they going through Your Parents to Get Too you?

This one is the best I've ever seen. Let me tell you why. Just a year ago my twenty year old daughter went on date with someone she met online, although they talked for a little while before meeting, they Skyped where they were able to talk face to face via the computer. My husband and I was not ready to meet this person unless she really felt after a few months that they were heading towards something serious.

To make a long story short on their first date, which they met in a public place. I was happy things seemed to be going well, since there was no upsetting phone call from my daughter saying that the guy was a jerk. This was a good sign because it meant that they were getting along in person and may have developed some sort of connection over a few weeks of talking on the phone.

While out shopping that morning my husband and I get a call from our daughter. My heart dropped as I was only thinking bad news. But surprisingly it was my daughter in a cheerful voice letting us know that she would be home soon, the date was going well. Really it was her way of saying that she was safe. I clearly heard her hesitating to get off the phone so I reached the phone to her dad who she then asked if he wouldn't mind speaking to the young man, dad had no problem with it. Now my husband and I were in the middle of the grocery store in the frozen food section talking to what we felt was a super guy, I remember it like it was yesterday.

Wow, none of the young men who have ever been interested in my daughter wanted to talk to her parents on their first meeting. This guy was a winner in our book, he impressed the heck out of my husband. Little did we know it was more of a plan to get our daughter to hurt her? From that day this young man was at our door every day at times I dreaded going home for fear I would see him sitting out waiting for us to get home, boy did he have a lot to say.

For a minute I felt like he was dating both of us, because he wanted us to know so much about him. I must say that we both were very impressed by his behavior and respect he had for her family. I could see that our daughter felt that she was not getting the attention that she needed from him. This was because the young man was busy getting to know her through her parents while appearing to be the perfect gentlemen.

Getting the parents to like you is an easy door to enter into if you are a commitment phobe because of a built in audience to help them with their lies. Now this does not mean that we were in on it, or are out to get our daughter in any way. Now the commitment phobe has more people to help convince you that their feelings and behaviors are indeed real no matter how sudden they are. But you should know that not every commitment phobe uses this route, in fact some like to stay far away from your family so that it does not open the door of return in which you may want to meet their family.

Don't be fooled by the fact that they are looking to meet your parents on the first date as something serious. This is just something that you have to pay close attention to since many individuals with commitment phobes learned the craft of making you fall head over hills for them. So how do you know if your date is interested in meeting your folks because they are just that into you or are they being deceiving? The truth is, you don't know, that's where you have to go with the flow of things, not making it more than what it is.

Does Your Family Seem to Love Them?

In the beginning we made time for this guy along with anything he needed. I mean he seemed to have more problems and issues then the nightly news. No, we were not looking for the perfect guy for our daughter because that really does not exist but rather someone who she can fall in love with and they grow as a couple.

The more my husband and I talked with him the more we saw that he had commitment issues and phobias. One minute he was in love, the next he did not know. One minute he was out showing her the world, the next minute he was broke. One minute he wanted her around, the next minute he needed space. This went on and on, not only did it confuse our daughter but her parents as well. Keep in mind we did not ask to meet this guy this early he wanted to meet with us to tell us how he liked our daughter since he thought they got along well.

We were just as caught up in the charade as our daughter was, we were able to pull back to see what really was going on. Besides him being a nut, he had major commitment issues that got in the way of all of his past relationships including the one with our daughter.

By the end of the week he was full of complaints, and very needy nothing like he was portraying himself to be to us and our daughter. I know for sure he was at least three years older than our daughter, we all took to his sweet personality right away.

I can tell you that by the end of the fourth month the relationship was over with my daughter moving on. His lies and deceit was getting the best of the whole family, suddenly he told us about his family background that was not good for him or anyone. My family and I learned a great deal from this young man, mostly how to detect potential prospects in the future. I remember before it was understood that it was final his behavior changed from night to day. This young man went from wanting to talk to us to acting as if he never met us.

His behavior upset my husband and daughter, it got on my nerves from that moment we urged our daughter to step back to take a closer look at this guy, that he was not what he claimed to be. He simply got tired of pretending and we got tired of watching.

The funny part of it all is that my husband asked to meet with him which he said, yes to. That day my daughter was getting dressed to go out with him after he met with her father, but that soon went downhill when the young man sat on our sofa and told my husband after a few questions about where he felt the relationship was going that he was no longer interested in our daughter. At this time only the two of them were talking in the room together. My husband could do nothing but get our daughter to meet with him so he can tell her how he felt.

At that moment I was more hurt for my daughter, but angry more than anything else. Shortly after I hear the door close, my husband peeks out of the window, sure enough he is leaving alone. Our daughter comes up stairs and repeats what was told to her father, that he wants to be friends. I could see a look of confusion on her face, but I understood what was going on. Our daughter accepted the friend request since it was awkward for her and he continued to talk to her through text and over the phone.

Now what we thought was over was far from it. He now wanted us out of the picture so he could do and say what he wanted to her. But we were not about to let that happen. I can say I am not the one to be messed with when it comes to my kids, this was the message he was sent.

My daughter talked to this young man for two weeks after the breakup he wanted her to go out with him, come to his house because he was sick and wanted to give her a gift. It was time to say good bye, which was the message my husband and I sent to our daughter. She had to be reminded that this person broke up with her in her home, now he wanted to spend time with her on the sly. Not in this life, as long as her father and I are still alive was the message.

She finally sent the message after the last request for them to exchange gifts. I remember she called me confused, I told her in a loving way that it's time to cut him off now. Our daughter and son know that we have their back, that we will never let anyone hurt them, so she cut him off. She sent him a text not to call her, text her and that she no longer wanted to be friends as he requested. She closed the door in his face to whatever game he was pretending to play. In fact she slammed it! End of story but I know that there are many more young women like my daughter who are taken for an emotional ride of lies and deception with a commitment phobe..

I was proud of my daughter for her strength to do something that I am sure was not easy, I commend her for that strength. Now she is living life, making friends, she is taking a break from dating, focusing on her goals and dreams.

I know this guy is out there praying on the next young lady with his extraordinary stories, mannerisms and respect for her family. For my husband and I the next time a young man or woman says they want to meet us because of our son or daughter I'm going to take out running.

What are the signs that they are coming through your family as a distraction from who they really are?

- o A commitment phobe is more eager to meet your parents and family to share their stories in addition to their interest in you.

- o A commitment phobe loves to get the blessing from the parents of the person they are dating to say that they are good for you by winning them over with their personality.
- o Commitment phobes are eager to please others in your family to show how loyal they would be to you by having your family on their side.
- o A commitment phobe has nothing bad to say about your family but tends to paint you in a bad light as if they are working with you because they are that into you.
- o A commitment phobe's story always changes, just as their interest in the relationship.
- o A commitment phobe lives in a world of lies and builds their relationship on half-truths.
- o A commitment phobe cannot be trusted no matter how sincere they try to be.

Just know that sometimes sitting back, saying nothing says a thousand words. If something is going on in your relationship that is not good or you need someone to talk to, reach out people you love and trust like friends, family member and pastor. You can also find a professional in the field to talk to or read self-help books to aid you.

CHAPTER 2
EVERY COUPLE ARGUES

If you are thinking that when you are arguing with a commitment phobe it will end don't hold your breath, because it will not. The more that person gets closer to you the more they will try to find a way to make you hate them. I know this sounds crazy, I mean who goes through the trouble of making someone fall in love with them only to want you to hate them later? A commitment phobe does, they do this to set the scene so that you two may not be a good match after all.

After meeting with the folks, once they get to know most of the people in your family who they claim to like, you notice later on in the relationship they no longer want to be around them. Who wants to walk around from day to day not know what's going on? I am sure you are trying to figure out in your head what just happened.

One minute they can't get enough of you, the next minute they are slowly growing tired of you and the things about you that they claim they fell in love with. It's time you know, people who have commitment phobias cannot and will not commit no matter how hard you try to convince them that you are the one. In fact the more you push the farther they move away because they do not like being pushed into a corner by anyone, not even you.

So what can you do to help yourself not become a victim of someone with commitment phobias? My best advice to you is to keep your eyes open and your emotions in check When you get that gut feeling that something is not right this is the time to set your heart aside to see what is really going on.

Having a disagreement is not unusual in a new relationship, this can be expected especially if two people are really trying to get to know each other. If you find yourself arguing about control, lies and disrespect than your relationship is off to a bad start, you have to pay close attention to what's going on around you. For starters having someone you are getting to know lie to you paints a very bad picture, it shows that the relationship does not have a fighting chance. It leaves more unanswered question about your future together. Below are a few flags you would want to pay close attention to in a new relationship.

- o A commitment phobe will not be clear on what they want out of the relationship. They are caught up in lying to you to win you over, rather than being real. They are in a wait and see mind set.
- o A commitment phobe will have more secrets than you can bare, but is unwilling to talk about those secrets to put your mind at ease. Don't allow them to see your frustration when you are not getting the answers that you want.
- o A commitment phobe will hide numbers or other things from you and if you happen to find them, they have no clue what they are or how they got into their house. Another trick out of the commitment phobes bag.
- o A commitment phobe can be loveable one minute, needing space the next. It's like they are short wired when it comes to relationships. Don't allow them to get you out of sync with your feelings.
- o A commitment phobe will tell you that you are the one they have been looking for to share their life with and the minute you don't agree with them they are no longer sure. Diversion, you are now aiming to please them.
- o A commitment phobe loves to question everything you do, but gets upset when you question them about anything. They want to be the only adult in the relationship.
- o A commitment phobe hides their phone, or keeps it locked whenever you are around, but questions you if you are not being open with who it is you may be talking too or texting with. Clear case of trust issues at its best.

In a nutshell, everyone has issues that take over their relationship from time to time but those issues should never derail your relationship or bring it to a standstill. Another point you must look at is if you find yourself arguing more than growing your relationship in a healthy way, you may be with the wrong person.

Are They Suddenly Secretive With You?

I have had friends as well as family members who felt that they found the right person for them to settle down with, only to be tricked by lies and games. Not all commitment phobe individuals keep your relationship with them secretive, some in fact go out of their way to introduce you to a very few select group of people in their inner circle. This is to convince you that what you two have is real. This is why it is so confusing trying catching someone with commitment phobias until they start pushing away.

No one likes a person who seems like they have something to hide, but looks at you as if they are going to take something away as soon as they turn their backs. Many commitment phobes feel the world owes them in some way for all of the crappy shit they had to deal with in their life. Now that they are in control of not allowing anyone else to hurt them, they are more likely to make someone a victim of love like they had been in past relationships.

This is more like the unpopular kid taking their ball with them once they see how good you are with it. A commitment phobe plows through everything they build in a relationship, than blames the other person for the mess they caused. When the smoke clears, a heart is broken into pieces with only the commitment phobe standing victorious, to put it lightly. They kill everything that has to do with love once you buy into their dreams, they make you a prisoner of loving them, leaving you with pure regret, no hope for a future. They watch you cry, beg, pleading for peace, to love them since they have your heart. The commitment phobe uses this to destroy any hope for happiness. You deserve more than this and should never accept this type of relationship.

Here are some of the things you must look for when dealing with a relationship with secrets.

o Are they keeping their phone locked whenever you are around?
o Are they looking through your phone but swear they were trying to put it on the charger so the battery doesn't die?
o Are they spending more time away from home with family and friends?
o Are they gushing over the new acquaintance you have not met?
o Have you been uninvited to an event that you were once asked to attend?
o Are they taking calls in the bathroom, backroom, back yard or while walking the dog?
o Do they go missing in the house, when you check the garage, the car is gone? You have no idea where heck they are.
o Are they trying to help you get out with family and friends to have to have fun so they can do whatever they want?
o Have you been sent to the store more times than you can count but, when you try to call home, no answer?
o Have they suddenly gotten a lot of new friends, whom they talk to all the time?
o Are they always on the phone with these new friends who happened to be the same sex as them?

Do they get upset when you question them?

Many times when someone is doing wrong they don't want you to find out about it because they are not ready to stop doing what they are doing. If you get that gut feeling that something is wrong in your relationship, the commitment phobe will not discuss the problems.

Questioning issues in a relationship is never easy. Addressing issues with an individual who suffers with commitment issues whether you know they have them or not is very difficult and destructive. Because a commitment phobe wants to be taken seriously as well as believed they want to be the first one arguing.

I have a friend who at the time was in her thirties dating this really nice guy for about nine months, but he never took her to his place, not even when they were not going out. He preferred meeting her at her apartment because it was easy, "For her." This is what my friend told me, he said to her on many occasions. I on the other hand was not buying it, something was wrong but she was so taken by everything about him that she could not see what the rest of her friends were seeing.

Who does that? I mean both are consenting adults, but one of them was not being as open as the other one. If he was not going out of town every other weekend he was too busy to make as much time for her as he did in the beginning. I can tell you that my friend really wanted to be married before having a child, she expressed this early on with the guy so that he knew where she stood that she was looking for more than a bed buddy. Everything seemed to be fine both my friend and the new guy agreed that one day they wanted to be married, not just dating someone to keep their beds warm.

It was very heartbreaking when my friend felt the need to follow him around on her off days when he started acting distant. The worst part of it all was, he would make her smile one minute, upset and crying the next as if it was her fault for whatever was happening. I met him twice and for me he was far from the real thing he seemed to double talk. I found him to be heartless, empty inside and antisocial. I remember telling this to my friend in the early stages but she just wanted to see where things were going, she felt that I was a caring friend who was just looking out for her.

I knew something was wrong I had seen this type of person in and out of many people's lives I loved. It did not matter if they were male or female their relationship always ended up the same, love'em and leave'em. That day she found out more than she wanted to know when she resorted to checking his Facebook. My friend was one that kept her private life private until a friend of ours suggested checking his Facebook page. All I can say is that she checked his Facebook and it was not good.

First of all he did not have just one Facebook page he had two. One of his Facebook pages was very simple, but the other one was very interesting in that it was very active full of pictures of him with women. All of a sudden when it came to doing things with my friend he was either broke or not feeling well. This seemed to be the case every time we all were planning a get together. After a while she even noticed but somehow kept the door open for him to work on their relationship. With each passing day he had less and less to say to her. She started to see that he was no longer interested in her the way he was in the beginning. In the end she came to the realization that her true love wasn't so true at all, so she ended the relationship a year later. Today she is dating but more as a friend and I know she wants a family of her own and my advice to her was to let things happen naturally.

Are They Afraid To Let You In?

This might be a little hard to believe but it's true that most people who do not commit in their relationships are afraid due to insecurities, fears of being abandoned and a range of reasons. There is no one reason why someone will lead you on, just to walk away unless they have commitment phobias due to past issues they have experienced or worst, witnessed. What seems like a great connection in the beginning of you getting to know each other can suddenly become awkward because someone is not being honest with their feelings. Sure you may have a million reasons why this person is acting out of character or maybe you don't. You are now left wondering what the hell is going on. You play the situation over and over in your head clueless to the fact that you are dealing with a commitment phobe. The truth is, it's them. If you know that you have been open and honest how in the hell can it be you?

Sure you are seeing, this side of them for the first time or it's something you have been dealing with for some time now. How can you have a disagreement over something like changing the channel? Or over how much food is on your plate? Or the fact that you said you will be treating them and paying for everything. What the hell just happened?

Are you starting to feel comfortable in this relationship? If you are then your relationship is soon to be over. As long as you getting to the love stage and not wanting to let them go this is when the show is all but over. Are you crazy, Johanna? I hope I am not crazy but I have seen it happen, the truth is that dealing with someone with commitment phobias is like diving into two feet of water, it can only end up tragic, but not for them because this is where they shine. Letting go and walking away is what they do best.

So what can you do? Hold back your heart until you see that you are not dealing with commitment issues. Sure they come off as cool, nice, confident and strong but that's the qualities they wish they had, you soon see them fall apart when you start believing it's who they are. Here are a few signs of someone who's afraid to let you in.

- A commitment phobe is not comfortable with their feelings. A commitment phobe does not trust but has no problem with telling lies since it's far from the truth.
- A commitment phobe will try to act as if they got it together. A commitment phobe needs to be seen in your eyes as the person who has it together even when they are mentally falling apart.
- A commitment phobe will always double talk. A commitment phobe has different endings for every story they have ever told you. If they tell you it's been blue all of their life don't be shocked when they tell that same story at your family gathering that it has always been green.
- Later conversations are more about them then us. A commitment phobe loves to gush about themselves.
- A commitment phobe is always looking for attention. A commitment phobe seeks attention as a way to make themselves look good.
- At the end of the day you are in control of your feelings and what people can do to you. You can't make something real out of something that's not there.

Below are lists of things you can do to protect yourself.
- Listen to what is being said to you. Again, I must stress this.
- Pay attention to events in their life be it bad or good.
- Hold back giving away too much too fast like your heart.
- Let them talk while you listen. Talking too much teaches a person how and what to do to you.
- Trust your instinct.
- Stop doubting yourself.
- Keep your emotions intact until you feel and see that this person is who they say they are which will take some time. So be in for the long haul.

- o Don't tell all of your secrets or desires too fast.

When all else fails instinct is your best friend, you should use it before you lose it. I have seen where people I know suffer for years in a relationship that is no good for them. They see the signs and red flags but they have lost their common sense in following that gut feeling telling them to leave, run, don't look back!

CHAPTER 3
WHAT DID I DO WRONG?

Have you ever asked yourself if you were out of your mind for dating someone who would not commit to you, ever? You've been questioning things in your relationship that have been said to you for some time now and still have not gotten the answers that you are looking for. A commitment phobe has no problem making you feel as if you are the reason the relationship is coming to an end. Knowing that you are not the reason for the breakup is important to not allowing the commitment phobe in your life to hurt you. When a commitment phobe is tired and ready to leave the relationship he/she needs a scape goat to be the fall guy for things not working out. They are no longer carrying or worried about how you view them, they see the relationship as over. For you it's not that easy and the commitment phobe knows this that's why they are able to place blame where ever they see fit. Everything you say now until they leave the relationship will turn into an argument, their patience for you has run out. The funny thing about commitment phobes is their acting skills, brilliant! You would never guessed in a million years that your confusion is connected to their inability to commit to you because they've made the argument about everything other than the truth. If you haven't noticed yet, commitment phobes are the perfect actors and actresses, they know how to make you believe in a lie.

Setbacks in your relationship when it is supposed to be growing shows that the commitment phobe has more control over the relationship then you expected.

One way a commitment phobe likes to stir up trouble in their relationship is by not taking your concerns seriously. Not being taken seriously can leave you with mixed emotions and a lot of unanswered questions, they know this. They have grown tired of the relationship so instead of talking to you about their feelings like any good adult would do, they start playing mind games. What a way to add salt to your injures when you only want to work things out, while they see no hope or future with you mainly over something that's not even worth an argument. Has this been happening in your relationship? If so it's not going to stop until they walk out the door, you have to open your eyes. It's only going to get worst as the days come and go you will end up being the one hurting the most.

You start to realize that their apologizes are not sincere, just empty words coming out of their mouth and it's killing you they won't fight for the relationship especially if you've been dating for a while. If you've only been dating for a short time your feelings may be just as strong depending on how quickly you connected to that person, you need to pull back. The game of deception is real and people play it out every day affecting the so called people they once claimed they cared for. If you are not careful you can end up in a vicious cycle by letting this person back in your life time and time again in hopes they have changed when in fact they would be saying nothing different then what they've said before. You desire better than this even if you feel they are worth fighting for. It's no fun if you are the only one fighting for the relationship, cut your losses and walk away. One of the best tools a commitment phobe can use in their relationship is the cycle of forget and forgive. Why are you afraid to open your eyes to see that this person has all of the problems with committing, and not you. The only problem a commitment phobe has when leaving you behind in the relationship is you waking up one day knowing the truth, which hopefully they will long gone by that time. Their fear of rejection is greater than their desire to be loved by you or anyone, so they keep you in a constant loop of duplicity. It's time to blow this joint and move on to someone who will be able to love and appreciate your worth. It's time for you to stop hurting and staying confused, let them go!

Spare me the details of being in love with this person you know is not committing themselves to you no time soon. Love should not feel like pain. Commitment phobes find comfort in making you fall head over heels for their lies. You end up with mixed emotions, anger, frustration, confusion and the list goes on and on while their sudden loss of interest in you has no bearing on them emotionally. They've presented themselves as everything wonderfully worth having except you now know this was not the case. You've damn near given your heart and soul to this relationship and for a million reasons can't walk away. Take a look around you and ask yourself if that person is with you fighting for the relationship? Are they just as affected as you are over the end of your time together? Could you be the only one that has this pain and they know this? Face it, you've given yourself, love and heart to someone whose incapable of having anything meaningful. They don't get it and never will, so with that said it's time for you to pack up your heart, sweat and tears and move on. You've given this person and this relationship way too much of your life. Their hope is that they are everything you want when they aren't. They wish to be the man or woman of your dreams but their short comings are so great that they can only pretend, for so long.

Only when you refuse to see this will you end up feeling as if your life or the love of your life has broken your heart. Realizing you are with a commitment phobe is the first key to destroying them and their behavior. Do you see a commitment phobe in your relationship? If so destroy them by moving on with your life. Are you a commitment phobe? If you are, time is winding down and pretty soon you will be on your way out the door looking for the next love interest in your life. When you take control over something that has been trying to hurt you for a long time by moving on with your life by finding someone that's real, you destroy the commitment phobe. You've given them their walking papers. You have to be pretty damn slick to out play a commitment phobe at his/her games.

Giving them a taste of their own medicine kills them and stops them in their tracks. As long as they feel that you are in like, lust or love with them it will never end. I can't tell you how many relationships I've been around where this has actually happened leaving the commitment phobe destroyed. If you don't have that better you then me mindset, you're screwed! Once you realize that they are not really letting you in is when you will see the truth. Trust me when I say that I am not trying to rain on your parade, I am just trying to get you to be watchful by knowing that you may have to do something you never thought you would do to protect yourself which is to fall in love with someone else while they stand by watching. Some will say that by doing this you are acting cruel, not so, you are protecting yourself. No one has the right to prey on your dreams and desires nor you with theirs. Have you really looked at what's going on around you or are you walking around with your eyes closed to this person. I am sure you don't want to hurt them the same as they have hurt you but life is not fair. Falling in love with someone who is everything you ever wanted and real is the only way to stop a commitment phobe and free yourself from a nightmare of fake love. Stop blaming yourself for not seeing things sooner, you see it now that's all that counts. Stop thinking and feeling you were the one responsible for his/her behavior, it's an excuse to keep you confused while knowing they are never going to stop or be who you want and need them to be. If your life support depended on trust and respect and you kept going into cardiac arrest because you received the opposite of that, wouldn't you go out and find the real things you need to keep yourself alive regardless of what happens to lies and disrespect.

You owe it to yourself to be happy and if you are not then it's your responsibility to find out what it is you need to make you happy. Why are you putting yourself through something that is not real? Nothing about the relationship is what you expect and if you cannot address it your ability to stop it or get out of it without getting hurt will be great. Give yourself a fighting chance at what you really want in a relationship if you know that the person you are with is not the person they claim to be. If you have to leave the relationship you should know that it is easy to do as long as you realize it has nothing to do with love.

If love is about respect and honesty and you have been battling deception and disrespect for most of the relationship you are lying to yourself if you truly believe that you are in love. If you do not face the fact that you may be dealing with a commitment phobe, I fear you will be dealing with his/her deception games for the rest of your life. Don't be afraid of being alone which means that you have to have a backbone in order to take control of your happiness. Face the fact, you may be involved with someone who is pretending to be everything you need. Please don't think for one minute that a commitment phobe will never get married, they do and they make their marriage a living hell. Marriages that have a commitment phobe spells *divorce.* It's not if divorce will happen but when I would like to think that people who are dating someone who shows signs of having commitment issues are not rushing to get married anytime soon. If you are dating someone who may have signs that they may not be the one for you my advice would be to run for the hills.

Do You Think They are Cheating?

Why is it that one minute you two are inescapable and the next you are taking a break. What am I missing here? Connecting the dots to a troubled relationship is easy to identify but connecting the dots to someone with commitment issues is like trying to fish with your eyes closed, you're not catching anything unless you are peaking. Still foolishly many people buy into these types of relationships almost every day even though they know the person is not worth it. Is this the reason why so many people are unhappy with each other and seek outside relationships to run to each year. If you are dating someone one and think they are cheating on you, leave now.

What is your partner doing in the relationship to make you think they are cheating? What steps have you taken to prove or disprove your suspicion? Have you talked with your partner about their behavior? Many times in relationships the other person will want time to take care of things especially if you are not married or living together. Don't take this as them cheating. Always ask questions and if you don't get the answers you want than be very observant to your suspicions.

I've learn many years ago that you can't date anyone while wearing your heart on your sleeve exposed to the world. When things become strange around you then the first thing people think is cheating. This is the commitment phobe's way of making you feel something in the relationship is not right. I know it's crazy and doesn't make sense but it happens, for control. Since viewing yourself as the most important person in their life in the beginning of the relationship they have now made you feel as if you are no longer important at all, what a creep. Don't be fooled by this behavior that is the way the commitment phobe checks to see if they still have you wrapped into them and their every word. So you said they have stopped calling and texting the way they were in the beginning and its make you nuts, you are thinking something is wrong all of the time. When you call them they are not picking up the phone and they are taking longer to text you back. Is this the commitment phobe who wants you to feel worried about the state of your relationship. Is this the one who is finding out that he/she is not sure they are having fun. Mind games and keeping you awake at night is the only way they have peace inside.

The commitment phobe's interest in you starts to diminish because there is nothing you can offer them that they did not lie and take from you early on in the relationship. In this person's eyes you are gullible and weak, too weak to be their partner because they have taken advantage of you. This is the mindset the commitment phobe has, which draws your relationship closer to the end.

If you are going through this in your relationship the best thing you can do is have a don't care attitude about the way they are acting, they want you to care. Caring about something that is out of your control only drives you insane, let go and get rest, they will come looking for you when they see you are not picking up your phone or texting them back. As long as you continue to make them feel wanted and needed they are not going to stop acting out for attention.

Let's take a moment to think about what you are feeling or maybe feeling right now. Cheating is a big deal in relationships, it's a deal breaker for sure. Nine times out of ten, when you are thinking and feeling your partner is cheating, it's true. Just what are you going to do about it if they are cheating? Are you misleading yourself in to believing this is taken place as a way to get that person to open up to you and tell you how they feel? It's not going to work if you are hoping they talk more. The only thing that you can do about it is pay close attention to their behaviors if they don't want to talk about it right now.

This is the commitment phobe's way of trying to end the relationship by making it seem as if they are no longer interested in you the way they were in the beginning. Remember when you date or marry someone with relationship issues you are going to have to deal with a lot of games and negative behaviors they take out on the relationship because of their fear to commit.

Is This Relationship Changing Me or them?

Why is your relationship changing you? How many times have you heard this from family and friends after meeting someone? The truth is that we all change at some stage in life for either for better or for worse. Many times your friends and loved ones can see when you are not yourself and have taken more of a negative mindset or your mood has become negative due to the changes you are facing in your relationship. Have you been feeling less focused lately? Are you feeling tired and run down after spending time with you partner? If you have answered yes to any of these questions then you are more affected then you think by the changes in your relationship. My advice to you would be to take a step back from your relationship by spending less time and focusing on things you want to do, take a relaxation day for yourself or just don't make time that day for your partner and see how you feel the following day. If you find that you are more relaxed, less stressed, and upset than your relationship and the commitment issues you are dealing with is taking a toll on you.

You never want to be in a relationship that changes your fun and loving personality to one that makes people stay away from you. Taking a break from your relationship can also help you relax and get back to who you were. Spending too much time with someone who is controlling, negative, and moody can affect your mood later on. Are you feeling upset or angry when you are around your partner? If so that is a red flag that something is wrong in your relationship.

Try to talk through your feelings so that you feel better later on but know that if your partner has commitment issues he/she may be willing to say less while you talk more leaving you even more angry. You should never stop living your life for someone in an effort to figure them out, don't feed their ego. If you are in a state of confusion and find yourself worrying it's your relationship. Everyone around you can see the hurt and pain placed on you from your relationship. What is going on in your life that you are not happy? How can you change how you are feeling? Do you notice that when you spend time with the person that you love they keep you upset? This is the case for many relationship where one of the partners has commitment issues. If you are expecting your partner, the person who has commitment issues to talk through what they are going through you can hang it up, they won't. Stop having your dreams and desires played against you by someone with commitment issues. You have to see that this person is a master mind at making you feel the way you do. Ask yourself this question, were you feeling this way before they came along?

You must remember that love does not hurt or make you feel like you are about to be alone. That my dear, is game!

Who you should be questioning is your partner since they have more than likely changed and not you. You will never get a clear answer to what is going on, just smoke and mirrors. If your relationship is to grow you have to be able to deal with the tough questions even if you feel it will stop your partner from wanting to spent time with you.

Never stay in a relationship that causes pain, hurt, harm and worry. Although most people have commitment issues you should never feel torn down or misused. If you feel this way clearly someone is taking advantage of you and it needs to stop. For goodness sake if you are upset and crying in a new relationship you could be looking at what the future holds for you if you were to stay with this person. Don't be so desperate for someone to love you that you put your own safety at risk or worst your heart. Learn to walk away if something or someone is not making you happy. These are just a few red flags in relationships with someone who has commitment issues.

Can I Help Them Let Go Their Fears?

How can I deal with this one, it seems everyone I know wants to save the world one man or woman at a time but let me be the first to tell you that you can't help everyone you date to think or act like you especially if they are not asking for your help. If you see that the person you are dating has commitment issues that are getting in the way of the relationship growing, it's time for you to step away before you are brokenhearted.

I am sure you love or have grown very close to the person you are dating or have married. You can't make them let go their fears and pain of past issues, it's their job to let go. You can't make them want to talk about what hurts them with you, it will never happen. A commitment phobe's thought process is different from you and I. They are protecting themselves first and their truth of who and what they are is never shared. You are just allowing yourself to be a victim for the sake of what. If a commitment phobe wants to talk they will let you know after they break your heart, when they say goodbye.

How can you help someone if you can't see you are being played by a commitment phobe? Helping a person with a commitment phobias in some cases can be stressful especially when you know that this person is resistant to you due to a long term relationship they don't want to be in. I have friends who have gone through this process, who were used and thought they can save the person they were dating from themselves and teach them how to love, it did not happen and the person ends the relationship for fear of being forced to love. What many people don't know that date commitment phobes is that they don't want to learn anything from them since they are not interested in giving themselves to you or being truthful about anything. Once they start lying to you they simply can't stop.

They have sized you up well before talking to you and know from their past situations where you fall on the hurt scale. They know what they can do to you to cause hurt that's why you have to get them before they get you. Staying in a dysfunctional relationship like this is damaging to you, so get out of this type of relationship today or you will end up fighting them to love and care about you.

What you really need to know is at the end of the day everyone has been hurt by a lover or two but when you are purposely going around wounding others for the sake of doing so you are only hurting yourself. Nothing is accomplished when a commitment phobe acts this way, you see them suffer because of low self-esteem.

If you are able to see the signs early on in a commitment phobe know that being in a relationship where you are loved to death in a sense of lies, betrayal and deceit is not going to make them or you better, it will make it worst.

Why do we feel the need to save a commitment phobe? What relationship in your past needed saving? Stop dealing with the past and get on with your life. Haven't you been through enough? When you are involved with someone who has relationship issues it's really dealing with a broken person who has never healed. One minute they are in and the next minute they are out. They never know what they want from day to day, people feel this way when married to a commitment phobe. There are times when you may see your spouse wanting to save the marriage and times when they could give a good got damn about it. Most commitment phobes are not looking for anyone at their level, they are not looking to be told what to do and how to do it by someone who knows what they want. They are constantly thinking of ways to get over on the relationship.

Below are signs you need to look for when dealing with a difficult relationship.

- o A commitment phobe loves telling negative stories about their past relationships. Lying is at the top of their list.
- o A commitment phobe is always cautious and non-trusting of others including you. They are always up to no good and are looking for the next relationship to jump into once they are done having fun with you.
- o A commitment phobe always needs some type of assurance from you that they are doing the right thing, like making you happy. Most commitment phobes suffer with their sexual self-image. A commitment phobe never likes to take accountability for issues in the relationship since they are looking to exit at the drop of a hat. Most start looking for the next person to date while dating you or married to you.
- o Most commitment phobes love to play the victim role for getting attention from you and others around you. They are always

hurting and someone has always done something to them to make them feel the way they do. *Big crybabies!*

o A commitment phobe is not in touch with their feelings and the feelings of their partner, you will never hear them say sorry for anything they say or do that ends up hurting you. Once they have pushed you to the end is when they say sorry. Their sorry is not real.

o A commitment phobe loves to keep watch over how much you are spending but will never allow you to say anything about what they do with their money. They are control freaks.

o A commitment phobe may be confident one minute and insecure the next. These mood swings are enough to drive one crazy especially if they are done frequently.

o A commitment phobe may feel the need to tell you what you can and cannot do but you are not allowed to tell them anything since they have things under control. They so want to be the Boss!

o A commitment phobe will get an attitude with you fast since they don't like to be told what to do by anyone. They do as they please.

o A commitment phobe loves to rush others but does not like to be rushed. It's a double standard.

o A commitment phobe loves to give the silent treatment in a relationship when things don't go their way.

o A commitment phobe will punish you by not talking to you or staying out late, not calling you or texting you when you don't cater to their feelings and their every need.

o A commitment phobe is good at promising you the world and seems to have all of the qualities you want after the first date, yet they never deliver on anything they tell you.

o To push back from a relationship they feel is moving towards a long term relationship, a commitment phobe will start complaining about problems with you that you never knew they had.

o When a commitment phobe is meeting new people around you they will mention negative things about you behind your back. This is to set the stage early on in the relationship for them to

make their big exit out of the relationship since it gives them a good alibi.
- o A commitment phobe is a good sales person and can talk to you about marriage and you being the one. The truth comes when they never want to agree on a set a date and any proposed dates they set with you are often passed with no mention of it. Kind of slick when you think about it.
- o A commitment phobe knows they are full of shit, they need to convince others of their feelings for you even if they are lies since the more believers they have the more truthful it sounds.
- o A commitment phobe will suddenly take time alone by using family and friends to get away from you. This is a sign the relationship is coming to an end and they just have to find the exit door before you see it.
- o A commitment phobe wants approval from someone even if that someone is your family and friends.

As you can see this list can go on and on since there is no set of rules when dealing with someone who can't commit to you.

Now that you are stuck in a relationship where you start to long for the commitment phobe's attention, and time, it's killing you that they are not looking to spend any time with you and that feeling is hurt and pain. Sometimes just opening your eyes is the best way of dealing with a commitment phobe since they can make you feel as though they love you to death but the longer you stay in the relationship the more you feel like they are killing you.

You can't make someone do something they do not want to do and this is true when dealing with a commitment phobe. Most commitment phobes relationships are built on disappointment, bitterness and lies which is how they see the relationship.

CHAPTER 4
THE IMPORTANCE OF TRUST

Trust is precious and it is something that you give someone you claim to love. However, not everyone is deserving of your trust. We all know someone we are cautious with when it comes to trust. Sure it's nothing wrong with giving someone the benefit of the doubt until you get to know them. The truth is everyone you meet deserves the benefit of doubt until there is a reason not to trust them.

Do you know what's the one thing everyone seeks in a relationship? Why is it important to trust the person you are willing to share your life with? Say you meet someone for the first time that you know very little about other then what they tell you. In the beginning of any new relationship, I always warn people to be cautions and not to rush things too fast unless you want to pay a heavy price.

I have found that people take what other people say about themselves as facts. I am not saying to comfort that person or to tell them that you feel they are lying to you but what I am saying is that you need to not believe everything that's said to you no matter who they are. By taking your time to get to know someone you will see what you need to see which will save you heartache later on.

Now why is trust important? Below are a list of reason I feel trust is important in any relationship.

Without trust your relationship will not grow. A commitment phobe does not operate in the mindset of trust.

Trust is having someone you feel you can talk with about anything. A relationship should be founded on trust. A commitment phobe will only give you what they feel you need and no more, nine times out of ten it's covered in lies.

It's impossible to build any type of relationship without trust. Many commitment phobes in relationships have no problems with building relationships off a ton of lies because many people are so trusting that they will believe anything they hear.

It's a sign of good character and love. A commitment phobe copies those good characters to enter and exit relationships at will.

You will not be able to have a successful relationship without trust. A commitment phobe does not care about trust since they know they will not be staying in the relationship long.

It drives one crazy if they can't trust their partner. A commitment phobe's job is to make you feel like you are crazy and confused while they are misleading you for their own pleasures.

Once the honeymoon phase of a new relationship is over, love and trust play an important role in loving that person or hating them going forward. This is not the concern of a commitment phobe because they will be out of the door before these issues come up.

Trusting is that sign in a relationship that says you have taken down the barrier around your heart and is now free of letting someone else have it. A commitment phobe will never give you their heart because they are too busy playing heart surgeon with yours.

Just because you are an adult does not mean you can't be conned out of your emotions. Most commitment phobia relationships are based on emotional love. Emotional love is catering to the person's needs and fears. This type of relationship is a death sentence and you are locked up since you will never get what you want and the person you are with will never be satisfied. You should know that once the relationship reaches its plight it will be terminated by the keeper of the gate who just so happens to be the one who can't and won't commit to you.

It will not be until later on that you will find their stories to be lies. Don't flatter yourself thinking a commitment phobe wants you in their life forever, they don't commit. They have played this game with many before you and they hold all of the cards. Commitment phobes love to double talk. They love leaving you with different stories from the last one they told you, they want you to challenge them so they can say you're changing because you trust nothing they are saying. Can you feel an argument coming on?

If you ever confront a commitment phobe you will see that they love switching up the rules. Before you know it you will find your self-esteem decreasing and your heart breaking since you are not allowed to confront them. They always want to be in control of everything because you believe everything they say and even fuss and argue with loved ones to protect them.

If you are not careful, you will find yourself with less family around and a loss of friendships. Sure some people may not want to see you happy but if everyone around you is seeing something you are not seeing and saying the same thing then it's time for you to take another look at your relationship. More than one story about the commitment phobes past life events should definitely be a red flag. Okay, come on how many times are they going to tell that story with different endings and not expect you to look up crossed eyed at them.

Do They Respect You?

It's been a while since I heard the old saying, "Respect is a two way street." Just the other day I heard this saying from a good friend of mine and, boy was she upset. It seems her new guy was not respecting her and she wanted answers from him. I clearly remember telling her that if she is not being respected she needs to take a better look at her relationship. I am more than sure that other things in their relationship were not working. In my opinion and based on family and friends who have been through this before, the best way to catch someone who has commitment issues is to confront them head on.

Why do the wait and see what happens approach in your relationship? Don't you deserved better?

How can you truly respect someone when you are continually being told lies? Do you know if you are being lied to? Have you felt something was not right in your relationship? Did your partner say something that made you question them? Are you afraid to say something because you don't want to upset, mess up or seem as if you have trust issues in your relationship?

I don't know how many times I have witnessed someone I love dearly fall for a commitment phobe only to find out they were not worth dating. A few weeks into their relationship the relationship was starting to show signs of commitment issues on the other persons part and later their actions and behavior was just too much for them to stay together.

Commitment phobes try to promise you things they can't and know they will never deliver on. The enjoyment of having you believe them is what keeps them lying to you. A commitment phobe does not understand the value of trust and honesty since he/she is operating from a different mindset, one on lies. In their mind you are the target and they are aiming to get you to trust them and believe in them while they feed you lies. This is the game of one who is afraid to give themselves completely to another person in return.

Below are signs you are dealing with commitment issues in your relationship as it relates to respect.

- o Being involved with a commitment phobe can leave you feeling run down and ran over in the relationship. Many times you are just too tired to deal with all of the issues they bring to the table.
- o A commitment phobe can have you to not trust your instincts when it comes to feeling things about them and the future of the relationship.
- o A commitment phobe goes out of their way to have you believe everything that comes out of their mouth by showing their emotional side that plays on your heart strings. *Stop falling for the ugly cry face!*
- o A commitment phobe can have you feeling off base with life situations whenever they are around. They make things hard and never have much to say, shy and out of touch.
- o A commitment phobe will say things that indicate you will not be a part of their future which can leave you feeling stressed and

worried about the future of the relationship. They can say for instance, I see myself moving to a faraway land. In this statement there is no, we. Did you catch that!

You can't force anyone to trust and respect you are even be with you so you should never feel forced or pressured to trust and believe anything they say. People will tell you that a commitment phobe does not respect themselves since they live in a world of lies and deceit. If you don't respect yourself than you are bound to be around people who won't respect you, it doesn't matter what type of relationship it is. Do you feel honor in this relationship?

How many dateless people do you know who want someone real and honorable? At the end of the day we all want this in our life in some form or fashion. The fact that not everyone will experience finding real love, breaks my heart. People who settle for any Joe or Jane that comes their way with a smooth talk will not know what they are dealing with until the lies start. There is simply no honor in falling for a commitment phobe who hurts you especially if they are unwilling to change their behavior and way of thinking .

There is simply no honor in being lied to, used and disrespected in order for someone to love you. When you are dating someone with issues like that of a commitment phobe you have to always take a step back or leave the relationship completely in order to stop hurting and being confused. The longer you stay in a relationship that is hurting you the more your self-esteem suffers. If you want someone to honor you learn to first honor, love and respect yourself. Learn to give yourself these gifts first and you will find that putting up with a commitment phobe who won't commit to you is a waste of time. Stop falling for the first person with a smooth tongue and good looks, it could be a commitment phobe. If you are not realistic with the type of relationship you are looking for, you will run into a fairy tale full of smooth talking and beautiful looking people with a ton of relationship issues. I know that no one is perfect yet you deserve to be happy. I just want you to use your head and not your heart when it comes to finding love. I also want you to keep your eyes open and listen for discrepancies when a commitment phobe talks so that you don't become a victim or victimize someone else's dreams.

Is Love A Factor?

Is love a factor says so much and has caused so much hurt and pain simply because most people don't understand what it means when it comes to being in a relationship. A commitment phobe will use the word love everyday like bait on a hook to get you or someone you know into a part-time relationship. Did you know that a commitment phobe can't show love no matter how hard they try. They say it but can't really show you because they are unwilling to be in love with anyone.

I've listened to many of my friends say they can't commit because of past relationships, hurt and pain or something they have seen or experienced growing up. Whatever it is it's no reason to lie about something that is so special. You are a unique being and should know that true love is never measured between your legs, your wallet or your purse.

A commitment phobe is incapable of giving themselves to love since their main goal is to get in and out of the relationship as quickly as they can. If you do become involved with this type of person the question should be what type of relationship are you looking to have? Although love is said to be unconditional it's really based on the other person's views of what love is to them and this is true for a commitment phobe. What you really want to know is what type of love are they looking for? What are their true feelings about you? And most important what type of commitment do they want?

Although feeling as if you are in love seems a little premature when you are in the early stages of dating, they are not. Love can set the course of your relationship like a guide in the direction you both are looking to follow if both of you are looking to commit. If after meeting your new found love you feel your heart is already questioning what you are feeling it is more relevant then you think. Many hearts are broken because someone is afraid to ask questions for fear of running the person off but it is through these questions that you get a better understanding of where the relationship is going.

Below are a few keys you can use in getting those tough answers to your relationship out of the way.

- o When you have something important to say talk face to face. It's never a good idea to text, face chat or even talk on the phone since things can be misunderstood. A commitment phobe needs to see your expression.
- o Look the person in the eyes when listening to them, this will help you pick up on what's true or not. Most times the commitment phobe, finds this uncomfortable and may look down at the floor a few times.
- o Don't be so fast to take over the conversation, give them time to answer. Putting words in someone else's mouth can only hurt you later on. If you don't want your last conversations twisted and torn to pieces then listen and don't help them out with word choices even if you know what they are trying to say. *It's not like you two are playing a fun game of charades!*

If you are not sure what they are saying ask them to repeat themselves but never assume you know what they are trying to say. It does not matter what your definition of love is as long as you are both able to communicate it to each other. I always like to ask people I know what was the last thing the person you loved said to you? What was your response? The reason why I like to ask this question is to show people that they are in love with the idea of being in love and they are really not paying attention to the development of the relationship or what the other person is saying to them.

CHAPTER 5
RED FLAGS

Have you noticed that people with commitment phobias display many signs that are direct? Maybe you like many others can't or don't want to see them because you are afraid of what you are seeing. You are afraid that the person may not be into you and prefers more of a physical encounter more than anything else. Also the reason why you can't see the red flags flying all around you is because you want your needs met even if it hurts you.

Do you know that there are many people out here that are qualified to be in your life but only one person is certified to be with you for life. Now don't get me wrong there is nothing wrong with dating you just have to know who you allow at your front door. When someone is looking to hurt you it does not matter why.

What does matter is that you take notice to what is in front of you before taking the next step. When you find yourself feeling uncomfortable in your relationship that's a red flag that something is wrong. Don't put off what you are feeling or picking up simply because you want a relationship because all your friends are in one.

Although people that have commit phobias don't want to commit to anyone they definitely know how to make one's life a living hell making it hard to break away. Have you noticed any red flags in your relationship? Do you know what to look for? Are you breaking up once a week? These questions might seem a little farfetched but let me tell you that they happen every day to innocent people thinking they are in love.

So now you are wondering what red flags am I talking about? Below are a few red flags that may be flying around in your relationship.

- A commitment phobe wants and desires being around your family more than spending time with you since it maybe something they lack in their life. They seem to have more fun with your mom, dad or siblings then with you.
- They also love being around your friends more than spending time with you and at times they act more like a friend then a love interest.
- A commitment phobe seems to always be affected by their past be it family or past relationships.
- A commitment phobe will become more critical of you in the upcoming weeks of your new found relationship now that they feel relaxed.
- A commitment phobe may start looking at your circle of friends to try to build some type of relationship with them outside of you since they know how long they will be staying in the relationship. Many times these friendships are with the opposite sex.
- A commitment phobe will seek to make you jealous over something that is small. That could be not spending enough time with your but with your family, friends or their co-workers.
- A commitment phobe seems to have an answer for everything that's wrong or right in the world and feel they are teaching you. It never seems to be a two way street in this case.
- Once in a relationship with a commitment phobe or if married to them they will try to keep track of your spending habits. Control freak!
- A commitment phobe needs you to do things for them but when it comes to working on the relationship, they start to complain.
- A commitment phobes story is always changing or somehow it seems to never end the same way every time they tell it.
- A commitment phobe has a hundred and one reasons why they are not inviting you to their apartment.

- o A commitment phobe who really has something to hide will go out of their way to keep their family and friends away from you by saying they live in other states or countries.
- o A commitment phobe has no problem being rude to the people you love.
- o A commitment phobe stops communication once they have convinced you of enough lies about themselves, marriage talk and you being the one.

When a commitment phobe starts feeling the need to exit out of a relationship because they have being around too long they begin picking arguments as a way for you to want a break from things or call it quits. Face it they need an easy way out and your constant nagging, is just what they are looking for.

Once they feel they have you where they want you a commitment phobe will no longer want your visits. A commitment phobe will pull back their wallet and spending on you quickly. You slowly start to see movie night and eating out stop all together. For the commitment phobe, there's just no time when you know you are not planning on staying in the relationship.

A commitment phobe has a sudden loss of income when they are starting to want to pull away from the relationship and expect you to cover the tab on everything. Are you seeing yourself in the relationship as an IOU?

Now that things are moving right along the commitment phobe in your life starts complaining about everything to get you to argue with them.

In a relationship with a commitment phobe you have no control over what is going on from day to day which means the commitment phobe can end the relationship whenever they so choose.

Now that the commitment phobe no longer wants to stay in the relationship you find out that speaking your mind upsets them when it was the one thing they loved about you.

As you can see these are just a few red flags I really wanted to share with you. The question now is what red flags are you experiencing? Now that you know what's going on, what are you going to do about it?

Distance

If you have not figured out the person you have been dating and feel like your relationship has taken a backseat then it has. It's really time to get your heart and head out of the clouds to focus on you.

Maybe this time the distance is what you both need but you keep pushing the fact that you are not bonding like you use too. To make matters worse you are not seeing that they have done this time and time again in the relationship, lied. It seems like whenever you two are getting along they pull back. This is a sign that you are getting too close and it's making them uncomfortable.

Distance is the only assurance that they are still in control of things most of all you and this relationship. So you rack your brain trying to figure out how to bring back the closeness you both had yesterday only to see that your constant efforts yield nothing in return, they are out the door. I have learned and have told many I know that sometimes you can want something so much that you end up not being happy later on and feeling like you are locked in a cage or worse dying. Don't you deserve better than someone just feeding you sweet words that mean nothing while promising you a grand future. Distance in a relationship can say a lot.

Not everyone sees distance in their relationship coming in a supposedly growing relationship unless you are dating a commitment phobe. The worst part of dating a commitment phobe is that you never know at what point your good times will come to an end in your relationship because they will never commit nor would they ever tell you the relationship is over. It's like dealing with someone that can never make up their mind in terms to if they want you around or away, either way you will feel it. Have you noticed that dealing with a commitment phobe is like eating a peppermint patty, one minute it's cool and the next hot.

I have heard the old saying distance is what makes the heart grow but in this case, it destroys it. Just because you are dating someone with issues of closeness doesn't mean you are dating a commitment phobe so it's your job to find out what's going on in your relationship and what's really causing the need for distance. There are many times when relationships need distance but that depends on the situation rather than the person's lack of ability to be real with their feelings.

I am sure you feel the room spinning around you while in a state of confusion when the person you are dating out of nowhere wants to take a break in the relationship. I mean who doesn't feel blindsided by this behavior? Look at it like this either something is not being said or there is really a lack in communication going on in your relationship. If you are not sure what to look for when distance is the major topic in your relationship below is a list.

An open heart is one of the signs to be aware of when the need for distance is being suggested or shown by a commitment phobe. It indicates to the commitment phobe you have fallen for them and they have not fallen for you. Lack of concern is one that shows that you are no longer on their mind. This behavior is the cause of many arguments. The commitment phobe loves to use this because it confuses their partner and forces their partner to ask questions. Needing them is one that the commitment phobe uses to run in and out of your emotions leaving you stunned and out of sorts about things since you are not aware of what's going on.

Feeling out of love is another one of the commitment phobes games they play because it makes you question them and chase behind something you were never given, love.

Lack of affection is another one of the signs the commitment phobe uses to get your attention and pull away from you. Everything they were doing and saying to get you comes to a halt. I mean who does that?

Now that you that you can see what's going on and why distance is being used against you, now is the time to pull it together and stop crying. Seeing you confused over their behavior and actions brings a commitment phobe pleasure. Why you ask? It allows the commitment phobe to know that they are safe in this so called relationship of yours since they did not lose their heart to you and your words but that their lies once again worked in their favor by getting them what they want and keeping their heart from pain and rejection. In the end this may sound crazy what I am about to say but it's your belief in what the commitment phobe say's to you and does to you that eventually ends the relationship. So stop swinging on their every word!

No Time

I can't count the number of times I've heard friends I know complain about spending the holidays and birthdays alone. When you are dating a commitment phobe you learn quickly that their time is only for them, you're on hold. Why is it that a commitment phobe never has time to spend with you like when they were getting to know you? The reason is they see the relationship coming to an end and you are no longer important, similar to a booty call.

Some commitment phobes seem to have to fly out of town with no notice to you and it's never when you expect it. Are you going through this in your relationship? What has changed in your relationship? Are you communicating like you used to? These questions are important to the future of your relationship when dealing with a commitment phobe. If this is happening more than you would like, it's time to have a talk with the commitment phobe in your life no matter if they are willing to talk to you or not.

You may find your emotions a little more on edge because you are not getting the answers that you are looking for in your relationship. A commitment phobe is not going to tell you what you need to know but will make things up they know you are going to accept. Their behavior is not acceptable and still many people stay in these types of relationships every day.

In this type of situation I always recommend stepping back for a few days where there is no talking, texting and face chatting to see where you want things to go. The more your mind is clear the better your judgment will be, they have you confused about the faith of your relationship which is a mood they use often to blind you from seeing what's really going on. See your time alone for a few days as down time to clear your mind and no matter how many times they call don't reach for that phone. If you live alone a quick text that states you are busy and will get to them soon will do the trick.

Isn't funny how in the early stages of your relationship you both had nothing but time to spend with each other. Where has the time gone? What is stopping you both from making time for each other like before? Maybe you are just over reacting and this is all in your head, maybe not! What can you do differently to make your relationship work and improve the communication is what is constantly on your mind. I believe in love but that's when you are dealing with someone who is telling you the truth and not what you want to hear by making themselves a great catch. Relationships like this are sure to tumble downhill fast. Never allow someone to tell you that they are the best thing you've ever had you must be the one deciding if that is indeed the case! Below is a list of ways to challenge your commitment phobe in making more time for the relationship.

o Say what you mean and mean what you say all the time. When it comes to a commitment phobe you have to make things clear or they will twist and turn your every word you say to fit their desires.
o Schedule your dates and time together ahead of time to leave no excuses for the commitment phobe in your life. If they start to cancel your schedule time this should be a deal breaker and you need to move on.
o Compromise when its favorable to do so and don't go out of your way making things work for the commitment phobe, they will only disappoint you in the long run.
o Deal breakers need to be set once you see a pattern in your relationship whether you want to or not, if not that pattern can end your relationship. It's like saying hello and goodbye to something new at the same damn time.
o Be real and keep a level head about things you can't control in your relationship unless it's a way out of spending time with you. When you do this it means you have to put on your detective glasses to see what the hell is really going on. What

excuses are they uses, I mean no one can be having the shits that damn much!

o Pay attention to every time a commitment phobe cancels a date or the opportunity to spend time with you. Is it always on a Monday, early in the week or the weekend? Is it just around the holidays? You have to open your eyes so you are not caught off guard by anything.

Once you can see and hear clearly what's going on in your relationship with a commitment phobe, you can look at things for what they really are and not dress them up to what you want them to be. Remember any relationship can have these issues but you are looking for patterns since that's what a commitment phobe operates by. If your worse fears are realized never be afraid to be the first one out the door!

CHAPTER 6
THE LYING GAME

No one wants to be lie too. If you are the one that's lying in your relationship, you need to stop. How did you feel when someone lied to you for no reason other than to control what you believe. Did you find out about the lie? Was it in a past relationship? Were you the commitment phobe that was doing the lying in the relationship? Where did it leave you in terms of trust and the thought of loving someone again? Consider that person's heart or are you that damn heartless that you seek to destroy innocent hearts looking for love. The best way to see if you are being lied to in exchange for your heart is to look at the list below.

o   Not so great job. After getting close to the commitment phobe you find out that the person you thought was stable and hardworking is really living pay check to pay check. Sure they dress nice but let me be the first to tell you that they have had that wardrobe for a while, it's just new to you.

o   Not being able to cook. Since dating the commitment phobe you have discovered they can really work their around a kitchen better than you can, thanks to their so called friend the one you no longer see hanging around anymore. A master of everything. You name it they got it and can do it but that's all to get you caught up into them, the closer you get the more you see nothing is what it seems.

o   The believer. The commitment phobe who seems to have every belief you have until questioned. When questioned about their views and belief system they don't understand the topic.

- o Family lies- The commitment phobe has either lost his parents, was adopted or raised by other family members, a closer look shows you that his folks live two blocks from where you are living. *Shameful!*

- o Always looking to get married. This commitment phobe is always shopping for a ring to surprise you. At a closer look you see the only thing that they are shopping for is your sex with no commitment. *Put a ring on that!*

If you want it to be over question a commitment phobe and you will soon see the truth about everything. If you are reading this right now, I want you to stop what you are doing and think about the things that are being said to you in your relationship that you don't like. Do you feel a connection to them? Are you allowing yourself to connect because you want a relationship? Where do you see this relationship taking you? These are the questions you must ask yourself and be honest with your answers since this is where you demonstrate how you are taking control over your life and your answers will guide you to what moves you must make next.

Needing Time

If you ever find yourself needing a break from you new relationship, take the break unless you are worried they will not be there when you return. A relationship with someone who is afraid to commit to you is exhausting because you find yourself babysitting the commitment phobe's emotional state.

The constant back and forth along with the I love you, mixed with lies that you catch them in can take a heavy toll on anyone after getting to know someone for the first time. No one should ever live in fear of their relationship ending when they are supposed to be in love. If anything one should want to work things out instead of giving up on their relationship something the commitment phobe doesn't do well.

If your relationship is draining you then you should take some time to figure things out, alone. I know dealing with a commitment phobe can be draining and confusing at times because a commitment phobe will find more ways to hurt the relationship before helping it. Taking time for yourself is the first step in dealing with stress in your relationship because it brings you peace of mind.

Below are things to do for yourself that will help you to relax when you are feeling overwhelmed in a crazy relationship with a commitment phobe?

- o Take time for yourself and do things that make you feel good.
- o Spend time with people who make you smile and give you less stress.
- o If you are home taking time for yourself, stay away from that person until you are ready to deal with them.
- o Rent a movie or read a good book.
- o Start a hobby or some type of outdoor activity.

At the end of the day the more time you spend with yourself the less affected you would be by the commitment phobe.

I Thought You Loved Me

How many times have you heard your friends fairy tale conversations about their relationship only to hear weeks later that it's a train wreck and your friend does not know if they are coming or going emotionally. Your friend is now more upset about the person not loving them instead of how fast everything took off to begin with.

Sometimes you are in a position where you have to ride out your feelings and emotions. I am sure this is not an easy decision for you but you need to investigate the past few weeks or months of your relationship to see why you are feeling the way you are feeling. Was it something they did you?

Was it something you heard? Was it something you saw that you can't stop thinking about? If you ever had a dozen questions for your dysfunctional commitment phobe relationship that you never got answers to then now is the time to address them with the person you love before moving forward. What most people don't realize is that a commitment phobe is unable to love anyone but themselves because of trust issues. Getting too close to you only allows them to pull back which becomes a cycle in your relationship.

You can go to counseling but many times the commitment phobe is not looking for help staying and leaving is played out in your relationship time and time again, it has to stop. The worst part about being in a relationship with a commitment phobe is that they will have you thinking you don't love them enough. You will also see how they are in and out of love from day to day, they are out of touch with being in love.

What are some of the signs you receive from a commitment phobe who wants you to believe that they are in love with you when really aren't, it's all a game to get you to give your heart to them in exchange for control.

- o A commitment phobe will say the right things all the time, not to mention they seem to somehow know what you need in the beginning of your relationship and does a great job at meeting those needs.
- o A commitment phobe becomes very understanding with any situation in your life be it bad or good. They are always willing to help put your mind at ease.
- o A commitment phobe seems to fall in love in no time at all after meeting you. They know what they want and they are not afraid to tell you but it is all smoke and mirrors once you really get to know them.
- o A commitment phobe is loving and giving, they have no problems with sharing their feelings in the beginning. But this behavior is all bait to get you hooked.
- o A commitment phobe is perfect in everything this is how you see them in the beginning once again they are playing on your desires and dreams for the perfect partner. *They are brilliant actors and actresses!*

To a commitment phobe they understand that marriage and love go hand and hand because they want you to feel as if you are the one. I am sure you have been told this more than a hundred times in the course of a week of dating them. What they are saying to you isn't real, they are waiting for you to believe it. A commitment phobe is an expert at talking a good game but it is it just that, all talk.

Once you see through the smoke and mirrors you soon realize that your relationship with a commitment phobe has been based on their lies and your sex and money. This relationship has nothing to do with love. Sometimes we want to be loved so bad that we ignore the red flags popping up all around us in a relationship with a commitment phobe. Has anyone ever told you that when someone lies to you and you believe them it's because it was a lie you once told yourself and somehow it's made its way back to you once again in hopes that you still believe.

We allow ourselves to be lied each and every day even when we know and sense the truth but why do we do this? We so caught up in the perfect relationship that many have mastered the art of becoming the person of your dreams. Why are we all living in this make believe world where we don't want to offend someone or walk away if we feel they may be full of shit? This is where you start to open your heart to lies.

We can't make the changes we need in our relationship when we live our lives through television and what it projects in terms of the perfect relationship. This is why your con artist known as a commitment phobe exist more than ever. No one wants to take the time out to be real and share their feelings or their heart for fear of having it torn apart and mailed back to them in a lovely box by a commitment phobe. Once more someone ends up on the shitty end of the relationship and nine times out of ten it's going to be you when you give your heart and soul to a commitment phobe who is not looking to commit to you.

My dad always told me if it looks like a duck and walks like a duck, baby it's a duck. The same is true for that person you are dating who you are now thinking is too damn good to be true. But if you still are not sure and not willing to walk away stick around and keep your eyes open it will be a matter of time before you hear the lies and see the red flags popping up all over your relationship. A commitment phobe will eventually show their true colors.

CHAPTER 7
ATTRACTION

Does attraction really matter when trying to find the right person? Just because someone is attracted to you and wants to be in a relationship with you does not mean they will give their heart and soul to you or even commit to you. When are you going to notice that they are not in love with you but the idea of making you feel as if they are? Sure there is nothing wrong with being attracted to someone as long as you are looking at the reason behind it. It's like this person who you did not know was a commitment phobe rushed into your life overnight and blew your mind. Although people you love try to tell you to take your time you are not listening.

Now weeks or even months later you are wondering if that person is still attracted to you since they are doing very little in the area of building the relationship. They are no longer paying you any compliments or sweet talking you the way they first did. What the heck is going on? Are you looking for attraction to run your relationship with a commitment phobe or are you looking for commitment? Either way you will not end up getting what you want in this relationship as long as this person stays a commitment phobe.

Is attraction the focus of the relationship? Sure you may feel days where you are in and out with your feelings now that you have really dug deep to see that this person you are head over heels for has commitment issues. But are you going to stay in the relationship? Don't you find it funny how every time you start feeling the need to pull back to reevaluate things in the relationship this person run towards you doing everything that they were doing in the beginning. The fun part about dating a commitment phobe is seeing how hard they work to get you to believe everything they say only to work just as hard to get you to stop believing in them or doubting the relationship.

A commitment phobe seems to compliment you in every way, never missing a beat which makes you wonder when you are getting close and desiring more time with them why are they pulling away from you? Most if not all commitment phobes know about the law of attraction and what it can do for a relationship yet they are against commitment. The law of attraction still applies to a commitment phobe because they are looking to be with someone they feel they are attracted too just like the rest of the world. It's their way of thinking that messes up their relationships causing the other person to feel rejected and hurt. I don't know how many times I have talked to women and men of all ages who are more focused on if the person finds them attractive or not, as if attraction will not allow them to get hurt.

Being with someone attractive is nothing if their heart is not open for love, honesty and commitment. A commitment phobes heart can be cold and dark due to fear and hurt. I am not telling you to go out and date someone you feel is unattractive but it's just one more area to look at when you are looking to fall in love with someone, attraction is not everything. When you are experiencing hurt in a relationship I doubt the last thing you will say is how attractive that person is.

You've Changed

Is everyone telling you that you've changed since meeting the love of your life be it bad or good? Do you find yourself stressed out one day relaxed the other? In your relationship do you find yourself happy one day, frustrated the next because of something that was said or done to you in your relationship?

Do you feel like they build you up one minute and tear you down the next? Do you find yourself saying you're sorry for every little thing in the relationship because they twist your words around? You have a commitment phobe on your hands.

The sad part of all of this is that I witnessed this a thousand times with family and friends but it never seems to change since a commitment phobe loves playing games. What's even worse is that commitment phobes love placing blame on others because they never do anything wrong, they think. They also love beating up the relationship emotionally which makes you feel like it's your fault. I don't know how many times I have witnessed this happening to my loved ones and friends it is a crazy cycle of hurt, pain and confusion.

The commitment phobe's behavior is nothing new in fact sometimes it can be seen as childish. It's not easy having an adult relationship with someone who is not looking to act as an adult. This is the main reason why most people are stressed out in their relationship when dealing with a commitment phobe. You end up with more questions than answers.

You can see the change on a commitment phobe quickly if you are paying attention. They chase you and pursue you like no other but once it's understood that you like them as much as they like you they start to pull back and lose interest in you. I have also seen where people lose interest for the commitment phobe they are in a relationship with only to rush back to that person in hopes they've changed. Maybe the problem is not the person you are dating, maybe the problem is you and how easily you lose interest when you are getting your needs met. Below are a few signs that are given when you are dealing with a commitment phobe be it male or female.

- o You are easily stressed out when your phone rings and you know it's them calling.
- o You pull back when you feel they need you more than you need them.
- o You are scared if they like you a lot and try to down play your feelings.
- o You feel safe when you are single because there is no commitment and no one to trust other than yourself.
- o Your fear to commit makes you feel if you do commit they will be turned off by you.

Many times commitment phobes feel this way and are afraid to tell someone about it. If they can't have you or won't commit to you they end up wanting to have you as a friend. The friend stage is the last resort the commitment phobe uses to keep you around.

Have You Been Excluded?

Many times you see women as the ones with commitment phobias but the truth is that men suffer more from commitment phobias then women. Lately women find themselves in a tough position when it comes to relationships because the men they date have so many commitment issues that they struggle to understand what's going on. I would like to jump right into the signs of commitment phobias.

- No one wants to date a single minded person. This is the mind of a commitment phobe.
- Many commitment phobes have a history of infidelity if they were married or in a long tern relationship you can expect them to wander.
- A commitment phobe wants space and independence all the time once they get the person interested and trusting of them.
- Commitment phobe moves fast on someone they want and suddenly loses interest when the person is interested in them. They are stuck in fear.
- A commitment phobe can be very charming, they seem to say and do whatever you want them to do which I like to call, the win you over phase.
- A commitment phobe is always romantic, they are outstanding sales people when getting their needs met.
- A commitment phobe shows very little concern about your feelings when you are upset.
- Many times commitment phobes have no problem with loving and giving you what you want and need in the beginning of the relationship because they know they will not be staying in the relationship long term.
- Many commitment phobes love to play the seducing and rejecting game to get you worked up and feeling sorry for them knowing that they will never commit to you.

There are so many red flags that should not be overlooked when dealing with a commitment phobe, one should not feel blamed for the outcome of the relationship that does not work, it's not your fault.

At the end of the day know that you don't have to be married or in a long term relationship to see red flags that say you are in love with a commitment phobe.

CHAPTER 8
NO MONEY

So now you are doing less in your relationship because your new love has hit a low in the financial area but a high in the sexual area and your bank account. Lately you find that you and the new love of your life are always home instead of out having fun, your date nights are no longer existent because someone is always low on funds.

If you feel like every time you turn around they are in need of money because they have none, then that's a problem. There is nothing wrong with helping the person you are dating but when they are not willing to commit to you why are you taking care of them? I am sure in the beginning of your relationship they seemed to have financial security, was it a lie to make things worse you are not able to trust them yet, your new love is not ashamed to say they need your cash but won't address the future of the relationship.

If this is happening to you I am sorry to say this is another red flag one that you must watch so that you don't end up feeling used and taken advantage of. When dealing with someone who has commitment issues they can end up making you feel like a fool by having you to take care of their needs more than your own. Trust your instincts by throwing this fish back into the pound where you found them. If they must hook on to something definitely don't let it be your bank account.

Soon you will realize that your new love may have done this more than once, their need is for everything other than you. You have become so blinded by the idea of having someone in your life that you look past the red flags flying in your face. You must ask yourself, why are they not committing to me? Is this the way they get your heart by making you feel needed? You find yourself going out of your way to prove to them that you are the one for them but you are being played in this relationship. If a commitment phobe wants to destroy their relationship with you, don't let them destroy your finances as well.

New Friends

Is your commitment phobe all of a sudden talking about their new friends? Commitment phobe's love keeping other people around their relationship because they know it will eventually cause issues. Just yesterday you two were spending so much time together, now you can barely get them to yourself. Overnight the commitment phobe has become popular with everyone you know and wants to go out and spend time with other without you. Do you say anything about it or let it go? Could you be over reacting about the amount of time they spend with their new friends? If you have not gone out of your way to get to know the new friends may be now is a good time to do so.

The commitment phobe is not expecting you to do this and may be taken aback a little. A commitment phobe feels comfortable in a relationship that has more than one person, they are not looking to be the one and only person in your life even though that is what they said. Are you feeling left out of their life now that they have other people to spend time with other than you? Know that whenever you are feeling is normal, you have to talk about your feelings to your partner whether they want to hear it or not.

Having a hands off approach with a commitment phobe is not going to correct or improve your relationship, communication will. Be prepared to have everything you say and feel turned around on you when you confront a commitment phobe about his friends. You should know that a commitment phobe does not like to be told what to do and how to do it by anyone.

If you want this relationship to work you have to be prepared to put in some overtime in the area of compromise. This is area is where the commitment phobe sees you, but they are not looking to make any changes with how they conduct themselves. The one that wants the relationship the most will end up doing the most work or making the most compromise, not good. You will have to stand your ground on how you feel if you want the relationship but be prepared for the commitment phobe you are dating to have a don't care type of attitude.

If you are the one doing all of the work in this relationship trust that you will end up feeling down about everything. You will not be in a good mood whenever you discuss anything of importance in your relationship if the commitment phobe you are dating is not addressing your concerns. In fact a little competiveness over wanting their time is what a commitment phobe thrives on. If you have not noticed this taking place in your relationship, look again. A commitment phobe loves attention be it good or bad. If you are picking up enjoyment from your partner as you express to them how you want to spend time with them you are not alone, they love it when you beg. Keep telling yourself things will get better in your relationship when you know that's not the case.

The only thing that's real about a commitment phobe is that they will never commit to you no matter how cute, handsome, established and sweet you may be. When you are working on issues in your relationship you will feel as if you are talking to yourself at times. Don't expect much in terms of ways to improve your relationship with a commitment phobe since they will have very little to say.

A commitment phobe wants you around until they are ready to end the relationship so you end up making yourself available while they make themselves unavailable, it should be clear what they are doing. You are not going to catch a commitment phobe at their game if you are making excuses for them. How many times have you had that heart to heart talk with them about the direction of your relationship only to witness them getting upset and saying that they need more time. If you know your priorities are not the same then that should be a red flag in your relationship that your partner is a commitment phobe. A commitment phobe will fight their emotions and feelings for you and will never commit to you even if you have a great sex life. Although I said that some commitment phobes do get married, you will know what type you are dealing with early on in the relationship.

Does this mean they won't or can't change? Who knows but at the end of the day if they won't commit to you it should not matter what the next steps are in the relationship. Clearly it's a wrap if you are looking at everything and not making any excuses for their actions and behaviors. The question is are tired of stressing and having a broken heart over them not wanting to commit to you?

Some people find it a challenge dating a commitment phobe since they feel they can change their mind. If that nut has not cracked all of this time what makes you think it will crack for you, not going to happen. When you date a commitment phobe you are at the mercy of that commitment phobe as far as giving you the things you need in your relationship. If you stay in a relationship with a commitment phobe that does not want to get married, you will likely feel as if you are being suffocated to death by the constant changes they will put you through.

Jealousy

Is your jealousy ruining your relationship? Where is that confidence you had in the beginning of your relationship? Has loving or dating a commitment phobe changed your life? It amazes me how quickly the new love of your life suddenly stops being confident and starts being insecure whenever you are around the opposite sex. A commitment phobe loves making you jealous when it comes to the opposite sex. This keeps things exciting for them and horrible for you, keeping a level head when dating a commitment phobe is what you must have if you are not looking to go crazy anytime soon.

Has your commitment phobe tried looking at a few of you friends in an effort to make you jealous to no avail? Have they canceled dates with you to hang out with the opposite sex that is supposed to be their friend? Is your commitment phobe seeking to get close to one of your friends of the opposite sex? Don't be fooled by their shy and innocent nature they have more games up their sleeve then you know.

Do you see yourself as passive in this relationship? If you don't then it should be a red flag for you because jealousy is not a good sign for a healthy relationship. When you are catering to someone's every need you end up neglecting your own needs. Who is going to cater to your needs in this relationship? Do you feel like your friends are playing in your relationship and your partner has given them the green light to do so? A commitment phobe is not going to make the relationship comfortable for you which you have to get through your head.

Do you feel that your commitment phobe has stalled in their actions in the relationship? Has your relationship become damaged due to other people jumping in and out of your relationship? Is your commitment phobe boyfriend or girlfriend jealous of how much time you spend with others but does the same thing to you in the relationship? The key to making a good relationship you can enjoy with a commitment phobe is to not take them seriously no matter what they say or how they say it especially when they are not committing to you now.

Never expect a commitment phobe to play fair or be gentle with your heart when they are causing chaos since they are never satisfied no matter how awesome you are in the relationship. Many times a commitment phobe will get married and make you think they are no longer afraid to love and trust but this is to not lose you. If this is the only way a commitment phobe can keep you in their life they will. A marriage to a commitment phobe does not change the fears that a commitment phobe suffers with on a day to day basis, they will still give you hell. A commitment phobe is not cured by getting married, marriage makes it worse.

CHAPTER 9
ARE YOU COMPLAINING?

Everyone knows someone who's a complainer. One minute you are in a very relaxed stress free relationship, the next minute you are in one with someone who constantly complains. Have you noticed how your new relationship blasts off with promising results in the beginning only to be followed by a breakup later on. Are you wondering what just happened? What could have gone wrong? The fact is that many commitment phobe's are big complainers since it helps them to get out of the relationship with you. No one wants to be involved with a complainer.

If you are not the one pulling back every time someone gets close to you, you need to question your relationship to see what's really going on. A lot of times commitment phobe's pull back because of their fear to commit to anyone. Sure a commitment phobe pursues the hell out of you by sending you flowers, taking you out, wining and dining you to no end while introducing you to family and friends only to pull back from everything they are doing when you become interested. This process can be confusing for anyone dating a commitment phobe.

Something clearly must be wrong when you find yourself happy one day and sad the next because of the constant mixed messages a commitment phobe sends you. A commitment phobe can really hurt you if you are not aware of how they interact in relationships, they can be hurtful and inconsiderate. They say one thing and do something completely different. No wonder why so many people go insane each year in their relationships. You are not going to understand a commitment phobe by giving a commitment phobe what they want.

Being in this type of relationship can be baffling for many leaving you in pain and fear of trusting someone later on. A commitment phobe can tell you they love you more times than you can count but that won't get them to commit to you. This is why dating a commitment phobe is not good and can feel like death for some leaving you bitter and angry.

Are you going out of your way to get to the bottom of those pressing issues that have taken over your relationship but your commitment phobe sees it as complaining? Many times when a commitment phobe does not want to talk about the future of their relationship they cause more arguments in an effort to distract from the ton of questions they feel you are forcing them to answer. They can quickly change the subject to something they feel comfortable talking about leaving your questions unanswered and you frustrated. They know they are never going to commit to you but hold you and your questions hostage. A commitment phobe will never settle down even if they happen to marry you, their minds and hearts will never commit to one person. Instead they will have you doubting yourself or thinking you don't add up to them.

The question you may be asking yourself when no one is around is why are you so attached to someone who is not that attached to you? Below are signs of someone with commitment phobias.

- o You enjoy the chase but not the catch or maybe that is the person you are dating.
- o You never stay in a long term relationship, never taking blame for the breakup.
- o You start out charming, seductive and attentive in the beginning of the relationship when it seems like you're in a relationship, you quickly lose steam when the other partner seeks out your attention. You are not looking to be attached to anyone.
- o You purposely twist your partner's words around to fit your needs. You complain every time your partner wants to spend time with you. Soon your partner sees you as clingy in the relationship. Name calling is another trick they love to use because it keeps you in a defensive mode.
- o You love pulling away from the relationship when things get to close. Distance is the only way a commitment phobe can stay in a relationship with you.

If you watch for the things in your relationship that can destroy it due to commitment phobias you are well on your way to not getting hurt in your relationship.

Always in Need

Have you ever noticed how a commitment phobe is always in need of something? Many times men and women who suffer from commitment phobias try to place their needs above others especially in their relationships. This seems to happen often in relationships. many people are clueless to what's going on in front of them. A commitment phobe's case for being in need is always based on something critical. This can vary from being out of money because they had to take care of something unexpectedly to an emergency yet they are not always eager to help the person they are dating.

If your need to be in a relationship is more than your need to find the right person who shares the same views as you then you are looking to be loved to death, with not commitment. This may not be the case for every relationship you enter into but if you are not looking out for your best interest then you will end up with a commitment phobe. Don't think that the sweet words, date nights, sex, flowers and nice dinners add up to the perfect relationship. If you are not looking to stay in the relationship long term you maybe be the one with commitment issues. When you make yourself the one, after only a few dates you avoid getting to know the person you are dealing with.

Commitment phobe's love this type of person since they go with the flow of things and don't ask questions until it's too late. If you suspect you are dating a commitment phobe slowdown when taking care of the things they want you to do and watch them throw a tantrum. Don't be that person who thinks they are in love before finding out who and what they are dating. Think before going out and buying things for someone you've just met or started dating. Your goal is to make sure you are dating someone who is looking for a committed relationship, when you start taking care of a commitment phobe you are teaching them to depend on you and your wallet even if the relationship does not go anywhere.

You are setting yourself up for something you will not be able to control later on. Do you think buying them will get you what you want? If you are looking to see if the person you are dating is looking for a free ride you will be able to tell once you pull back your money.

When you are in a relationship with a commitment phobe you end up giving more and getting nothing in return. Try getting to know the person before going into your bank account to shower them with nice and expensive gifts. Learn to save your gift for later on in the relationship once you are sure this is something you both want. If you find yourself trying more and giving more in order to be loved by someone who does not understand love you are fooling yourself. Now that you have stopped spending your money on the relationship have you noticed they are no longer interested or become very short tempered when you start talking about a long term commitment. A relationship that's not built on trust and love will eventually be over before you know it.

If you are not familiar with someone who is always in need and wants to use you in your relationship, below are a list of things to watch out for.

o   They will call you at all times of the day talking about what they have and don't have in hopes that you will offer assistance. A commitment phobe will not just come out and say they need your help, they will let you offer first.

o   A commitment phobe will go from paying for everything in the beginning of the relationship to taking a backseat once they see you are more interested in a relationship with them.

o   They are always telling you things they want to do for you when they get paid but once their payday comes they are nowhere around,.

o   A commitment phobe will use anything they can to get you to argue with them so that they can get out of a relationship with you if they are not getting the attention that they need. More and more relationships are becoming affected by people with commitment issues. Trying to get a commitment phobe to see that they have serious issues is like trying to convince yourself that you can fly.

Once you start to understand the mind of a commitment phobe you begin to look at your relationship with this person differently. Either you see yourself with this person or not. Dating and loving a commitment phobe is not easy and your relationship is plagued with their fears and lack of change from the beginning.

Understanding that your view of what a relationship is and what the commitment phobe's view of what a relationship is may be the same. The only thing that makes any difference in the relationship with a commitment phobe is if what they believe is something they can see themselves doing in a relationship and many can't. It's because of this reason why relationships with commitment phobes don't last long and end in hurt and pain. A commitment phobe has to be willing to make real changes in their thought process and actions, if they want the relationship to work or you might have to walk away if they don't. I am sure you can find a hundred reasons why you shouldn't give up on your relationship but the truth is if they have not changed all of this time, it's not going to happen. You have control over what hurts and causes you pain this is one area that most people do not pay any attention to. You have to be willing to do what's best for you even if that is staying in a relationship with a commitment phobe or walking out of one. The choice of being loved to death is simply up to you so don't be afraid to make a decision.

No More Marriage Talk

When was the last time you talked about marriage? Are you still seeing this person as the only one for you even though you know they have issues with commitment. How many times have you been in a relationship where the person comes in knowing what they want and is ready to settle down only to have a change of heart later on? These are red flags in dating that many people do not pay enough attention to. What about the commitment phobe that sets the wedding date only to change it every time you have an argument. The crazy part about these situations is as long as they are happening to you you're at a loss to what's really going on in your relationship, it's when you sit down with yourself that it's clear you have a commitment phobe on your hand.

How can this person be at every level in life that you are on yet have a fear to commit? More importantly have you found your match in life? The person you should want to be with needs to want the same things out of life that you want, or it won't work.

Now that you are no longer talking marriage the person you thought was into having a long term relationship with you is going back and forth with their feelings. Their fear to commit has taken over your entire relationship and you feel it in every argument. If you want your love to last with a commitment phobe they have to be willing to grow and make changes in the best interest of the relationship. Don't be the one talking about marriage but never making it to the Alter. If marriage is where your heart really is than you have to do some soul searching about the fate of your relationship with a commitment phobe.

I know people who never make it down because they fear that they are not enough. I remember a time when my good friend who was dating this nice guy who promised her everything under the sun including marriage, something she really wanted. They had been dating for two years, she was tired of talking about getting married and planning an off and on wedding due to their issues and his failure to commit. It's obvious that when it came time to planning the wedding and talking to people about the ceremony her boyfriend would find a way to pick an argument, he always took away from her being happy. It was clear he was not honest about wanting to marry her and could not say it for fear of her breaking up with him.

They eventually talked about everything and he came clean with his feelings of not being ready to get married. She was devastated since she had put so much into the relationship but the signs were there the entire time that he was a commitment phobe but she did not want to see it. She realized he was playing games and stringing her along for the last two years, so she left the relationship.

Today she is happily married and thanks god that she was able to walk away from something she had invested so much time into, but that did not mean her any good.

Below are signs that say your relationship will not make it to the Alter.

- A commitment phobe is always looking for the next relationship while still involved with you.
- A commitment phobe is great salesperson. They are not in touch with their inner truth which makes it easy for them to lie to you.
- A commitment phobe will never show you their emotions but they love feeding off of your emotions.
- A commitment phobe will promise you the world including marriage, but they will never deliver on it. If they do get married they will make you pay for it through keeping you unhappy.
- A commitment phobe is always affected by their past relationships that had a negative impact on their life no matter how good your relationship with them may be.
- If you are stuck in a relationship with a commitment phobe they will keep you confused in order to control the relationship

Know that nothing is worth making your life sick over especially when it comes to dealing with another individual who mistreats you. A commitment phobe will keep you looking through smoke and mirrors until they are ready to walk away from the relationship, however long that is.

If you are the commitment phobe and feel that you have found the right person for you the best thing that you can do is to face your fears about commitment and be honest to the person that you claim to love. Find a way to make it work even if that means you may need to talk to someone about your feelings when it comes to relationships.

It's important for you to understand why you are feeling the way you do or why your partner is feeling they can't commit. Everyone has dealt at some time in their life with commitment issues so knowing that you are not the first person and won't be the last person who fears commitment should not stop you from getting what you want out of life. Read books that help you deal with relationship fears. If you suffer with anxiety practice mind meditation to help you relax in your relationship.

Sometimes talking to a good friend or someone you can trust about your fears when it comes to relationships can help you see things clearer. Relationships and talks of marriage can bring on stress even if that stress is good. You don't have to be afraid to give your heart away to someone, just know who you are dealing with. Don't be quick to jump into a relationship because you feel alone. Being alone is not a good reason to grab anyone and make them that special person in your life.

CHAPTER 10
KEEPING THE PARENTS AWAY

Have you ever met someone who gets along so well with your parents that's its shocking? They seem to talk about everything, you find that your folks truly like them. Now that you have grown in your relationship the relationship your partner once had with your parents has hit a bump in the road and you're not sure why. Lately they have not been as nice to them as they once were and when family events are over you are caught in the middle of their disagreements.

Why is this happening? You feel stuck in the middle of the people that you love the most. Once more you are not in the mood to pick sides so you say nothing. Saying nothing is not going to change what's going on in your relationship. Many times the best way to get to the person you love for a commitment phobe is to attack their parents or someone they love. Is your commitment phobe wanting you to pick them over someone that has been a major part of your life? If so this is a problem, one that you must do something about fast or you will have more problems in your relationship. A commitment phobe loves seeing the frustration on your face when it comes to something they are influencing. Now that they have the family in an uproar they can sit back while playing both sides against each other. They carefully plan to have your family members at each other which keeps everyone distracted from seeing them for who they are, a commitment phobe. Still you say nothing while watching your folks go out of their way to make this person you feel that you love, feel special.

I had a friend whose mother and father liked the man she was dating only to have him turn their family upside down with a bunch of allegations that they did not like him soon, they wanted him out of the family. While this was happening he was using everyone against each other and causing his girlfriend to pick his side, what a creep! A commitment phobe will put a lot of hard work into making life a living hell in your relationship by lying, then will get mad at you for not believing in them. This person wanted to be a part of the family and wanted everyone to treat him as such. This was the weapon he used to keep everyone at each other while making demands, what a jerk!.

What she did realize, when she was able to calm her boyfriend down, was that he was extremely jealous of her relationship with her parents. This is where one can see the breakdown of the commitment phobe since they are always craving attention and when they don't get it, the gloves come out.

It got to where a year and a half into their relationship, she was not happy. This guy competed for her attention not only with her family but even with the family dog, nothing was off limits. If he was not criticizing the food she prepared for him he was on the side making snide remarks. This behavior brought into question if he was really serious about commitment since he was doing everything to upset everyone. For two he put her through so much because of his fears to commit. Everything came to an end a few months ago when she had had enough of his behaviors and whining.

She eventually realized he wanted her to himself which he had but did not know how to commit. Walking away from this two year relationship was the best thing she's ever done for herself. Sometimes it makes me wonder why so many beautiful people are single and then I think of commitment phobes taking up peoples time who really want to connect.

Below are things commitment phobes do in their relationships when they know they are about to leave you.

- o A commitment phobe shows you that they get along with everyone you introduce them to only to turn against them later on..
- o A commitment phobe will praise your family one minute and tear them down the next. Who cares how they feel, they're out the door anyways.

- A commitment phobe takes everything you say personal and uses it against you and the relationship.
- A commitment phobe becomes jealous of family and friends once they get to know them.
- A commitment phobe wants you to spend less time with the people you love and more time with them. They want you to abandon those you love. Isolation at its best.
- A commitment phobe will find as many reasons as they can to put down your family and friends once they get to know you. They are never happy. This is to make you upset to leave them.
- A commitment phobe will tell you say one thing and do something else.
- A commitment phobe will have you pushing people you talk to away so the only person that you have in your corner is them.
- A commitment phobe is never comfortable at your family gatherings because of their ill feelings and all of the hell they've caused.
- A commitment phobe will not make themselves available to the people you love.
- A commitment phobe finds reasons to argue with you and those around you. They are forever wanting you to choose their side.
- A commitment phobe will make your family and friends out to be the bad guys every time things go wrong.
- A commitment phobe expects you to spend all of your time with only them. They love chaos.
- A commitment phobe will lie about things that never happened to keep you confused.
- A commitment phobe will want to convince you that your folks are not happy about your relationship.
- A commitment phobe is only interested in stringing you along until they've had enough of hurting you and causing you pain. They have a better you then me attitude.
- A commitment phobe will start to take advantage of you sexually and financially.

No one likes someone who is always down and out when they can't get their way, this is true for a commitment phobe, they are sore losers. If they are not the only one making you happy then they have a problem with anyone else who is. They are very hurt and wounded souls who may be aware of their behaviors or not either way you have to protect your heart from these types of relationships.

Double-Talk

Have you ever met a person who double-talks? If you have ever been in a relationship with a commitment phobe you probably have experienced this a few times. They tell you one thing only to change it as the day goes by. Their story forever changes, they go from wanting a short term relationship to wanting a long term one in the matter of minutes, days or weeks. They are freestyling their way into your heart with all of their fears. It makes you question what to believe when they start talking. Dealing with a commitment phobe is frustrating and leaves you angry many times.

They always say misery loves company and commitment phobes love having others feel what they went through. Somehow they have convinced you that everything they told you in the beginning of your relationship has changed and you fall for it hook, line and sinker. Not to mention that that story they told you about their parents dying when they were young was one big fat lie, I know it's awful. Then you find out that their parents are alive and well and live a few blocks from where you live. As you can see, there is no limit to what a commitment phobe will do to get you to trust and believe in them. Sad stories seem to work the best at getting them what they want. Needing answers to why they lie to you in the first place, they continue piling on more lies one after the other beginning from the last lie they told you. For good measure you listen hoping to hear why they lied, still you are too blind to see through what they are saying to you.

Everything about their life you now realize was just lies to get you to feel sorry for them. Now you are questioning everything they've ever told you, about their family, friends, and career. What else could they be lying about? A commitment phobe will never tell you what you need to hear if they are not looking to commit to you, they will tell you what sounds good and believable. Hell you are just finding out that their friends weren't' real. Why do people do this to others? This is what many like you think and feel. One minute they are talking marriage then the next minute they are nowhere near ready for marriage, at least that's what they are telling you now, so which one is it? Are you just as confused as I am, right about now?

Don't be since you know what they are doing and why they are doing this. Your believing their lies is not going to make a commitment phobe want to settle down with you. One minute they are talking about wanting kids the next minute they can't think of having kids in this world. Something is always changing with them and nothing is what it appears to be.

Dealing with a commitment phobe can be confusing I am sure but you don't have to stay confused by the things they say or do. At times they can make you feel as if you are losing your mind. If you've ever questioned a commitment phobe you know it was not easy, in fact they displayed a confusing look on their face as if they had no clue to what you were angry about. When you really look at the relationship with a commitment phobe for what it is you learn that you've invested in nothing but someone whose selfish behavior has caused you hurt and pain. Below are signs you may be dealing with in a commitment phobe relationship.

- o A commitment phobe will say thing in the beginning of a relationship and not remember one word of it later on.
- o A commitment phobe never wants you to know the truth and for this reason do they constantly change their story.
- o A commitment phobe will match what your needs are in terms of relationship. For instance if you are wanting to get married one day they are looking for the same thing, it's not until you show your emotions that they are no longer interested.
- o A commitment phobe will give mixed messages throughout the relationship as a way to keep you frustrated and confused.
- o A commitment phobe is always changing their needs. One minute they want intimacy, the next minute a commitment phobe needs space.

- One minute they love animals, the next a commitment phobe is allergic to them and can no longer be with you.
- One minute a commitment phobe wants to move in with you, the next minute they forgot that they love living alone. They love making up excuses for everything.
- A commitment phobe will start out with very few friends only to end up with friends you never knew they had.
- A commitment phobe will have money in the bank but want to spend yours first. They start looking for other areas in the relationship where they can take advantage of you.
- A commitment phobe will make an argument out of anything to have a reason to end the relationship. Such as not having enough toilet paper on the roll.
- A commitment phobe will never have the same story twice and if they do it's something they just remembered. They can also be seen as a taker.

Emotional Abuse

Have you ever noticed that when things do not go the way the commitment phobe in your life wants it, they can be very abusive? In fact they will blame you for everything that goes wrong in the relationship and if you are not careful you would end up believing it. If you are not the reason for their feelings I am sure they will look back far back enough in their past to find something that would do the trick. Can you see how this type of person is harmful to your life? Can you see how they can cause you so much damage that you stop loving and trusting others? It's no wonder you have not lost your mind in all of the relationships you've had with commitment phobes.

I've learned that broken relationships lead to broken hearts and those hearts end up hurting others they come in contact with if they are not careful. What type of abuse are you dealing with in your relationship? Have they said they were sorry a dozen times only to do it again? One of my family members where involved with someone who was more into hurting them then being truthful about their feelings. They fought and did things to hurt each other time and time again. It was the only way this person can deflect from what they were doing without being obvious.

The real reason why commitment phobes become abusive in their relationship has nothing to do with you but more to do with them feeling the need protect themselves from love, commitment and getting hurt, now where does that leave you?

No one should stay in any relationship that hurts them mentally or physically. Loving someone should not feel like a battle. Thinking about what you want out of your relationship if you are with a commitment phobe is the best way to make the necessary steps towards walking away. I would never tell someone to walk away from their relationship, but if you are dealing with a commitment phobe and things are not getting any better you may have to leave.

The sad truth is that many people never make it out of these types of relationships and end up scarred for life. The longer you stay with a commitment phobe who does not want to commit to you, the more you risk becoming just like them. Don't live your life in a relationship where you become broken pieces of the person you once was. You become the scape goat in the relationship. Can you say I had nothing to do with their childhood or last relationship issues? Can you also say I am not the person who abandoned them in life? You are not responsible for all of the bad things that happen in their life, don't you ever except that.

You will never know what baggage someone is carrying around until they allow you to get close enough to see and by this time you have seen more than you wanted to see. This is why I also say it would be nice to see packaging information on someone's forehead you are thinking about dating. What would appear on the forehead would be, "Approach with caution, this individual may have the tendencies to isolate you, blame you or become critical of you, threaten you the more you get to know them." Since this is not the case you have to be aware of the actions and behaviors of the person you are dating or interested in and hold them, not yourself accountable for what happens.

Every second of the day someone you know may be dealing with a commitment phobe and is too ashamed to say anything about it. You never have to feel that in order to have love you must become angry, bitter, heartbroken, disrespected and humiliated for someone to truly love you. You also don't have to stay in a relationship that does not value you as a person and that keeps you emotionally broken and confused from day to day. Below are a few signs and tricks used by those who seek to turn you into a victim.

- o Demeaning - You feel humiliated as your character is attacked. You try to speak up for yourself in the relationship only to be put down and ignored.
- o Gas lighting - You are given false information by the commitment phobe while your abuse claims in the relationship are denied making you look as if you are going crazy, out of your mind.
- o Isolation – You are made to feel guilty for spending time with family and friends. You are also made to feel guilty for doing anything that you love that keeps you happy. A commitment phobe loves to control others.
- o Criticizing – You feel as if you never do anything right in their eyes and are put down by their words. Your shortcomings are the highlights of the conversation more than anything else. .
- o Blaming – You are never right on anything, you are made to feel as if everything is your fault when you know it's not. A feeling of helplessness takes root.
- o Threatened – You never feel safe in your own relationship and live life on eggshells for fear of losing the one and only person you love who doesn't love or give a damn about you.
- o The Silent Treatment – You are ignored when you do speak up. It's enough to stop you from talking, mission completed. You feel as if you are being punished for speaking your mind, you are.

It's never easy staying in a relationship with someone whose promised you the moon and stars yet you're still waiting on that delivery. Face it you are with a commitment phobe who has issues with commitment which is not your fault. So why are you punishing yourself for someone else's way of thinking? Stop allowing yourself to be victimized while waiting on love to show up at your door. Below are a few positive keys you can use to take control of your life and get your emotions back on track.

- o Know who you are dealing with – A commitment phobe will come across as sweet, loving and understanding but deep down they are far from it, they are really just a copycat of something they use to be, something you wanted before they got hurt.

- o Trust yourself – Don't look to someone else's truth as your own nor their promises as good faith for putting up with hell. Answer your phone to your heart and step away. Even when you don't want to acknowledged something is wrong your inner soul has already given you the answers, will you listen. Trusting yourself if the first sign of self-love.

- o Forgive yourself – The second sign of loving yourself is to forgive your mistakes just as you would others. Pay attention to this moment in your life because it has brought you to the point you're at today. We all make mistakes from time to time but forgiving yourself is the only way you can move on to a better you. You can't save everyone and risk losing yourself in the process.

- o Break Free – It's never easy giving up on someone you had an inner investment in but when love hurts and burns, it's time to jump up and move on. Loving someone is never meant to destroy or dehumanize you.

- o Know your worth – See yourself as someone who is deserving of real and true love and not a counterfeit version. Loving someone is not supposed to destroy you in the process, you never should feel as if it's your responsibility to make a bad relationship work? The only responsibility you have is to yourself and your happiness. Make sure when it comes to relationships that you are giving and receiving the same in return.

How long are you going to blame yourself for someone else's actions? You should know that whatever happens in your relationship is not your fault alone, it takes two to make something work and one to destroy it. Something inside of you should be tapping on your heart to move on, if you can't save yourself, try saving your heart. How long are you going to deny yourself someone who deserves you?

How long are you going to ignore your truth? These are questions you should be asking yourself if you are in a relationship with a commitment phobe whose not valuing you, but victimizing you. You should never feel alone or scared to leave a bad situation.

CHAPTER 11
BLOCKING DISTRACTIONS

Now that you've decided to work on your relationship with a commitment phobe be prepared for there to be interruptions in the area of emotional issues. It will be as if your relationships has become one that suffers from a case of ADHD since the commitment phobe will be more high strung than ever before. To make things worse you will not be able to do anything right in their eyes, despite your constant efforts to make things work. They will do everything in their power to work against your efforts leaving you defeated, emotionally and mentally especially if they are not willing to change.

A commitment phobe has many ways to distract you from what they are doing. Many times these distractions take the form of arguments, being needy and expressing to you just enough to hold you hold off their back about committing. If these distractions don't work, they tend to make you jealous of friend of the opposite sex in hopes that it takes away from you wanting answers about the future of the relationship, which they are not happy to talk about. When you find yourself catering more to the needs of another person than your own in the relationship then it's time to take a step back, you're too close. Stop sacrificing who and what you are for something that is not real. Why are you being distracted with everything but the truth? Have your disagreements somehow gotten off track on something that makes no sense? If the answer is yes, you are being distracted by a commitment phobe in your life. Just because you don't play such games does not mean no one will not play with your heart and mind. I understand that not everyone is going to give up on their commitment phobe relationship. There are many signs that a person gives when they are dealing with commitment issues in a relationship. The key is if you are paying attention when they are in your face. I have witnessed many of my friends in relationships with commitment phobes struggling to understand where to place their feelings and emotions that are not being acknowledged. No one can buy love and affection through making yourself a doormat in a relationship with a commitment phobe. When you are tired and want answers it never comes or ends the way you want it to. You will look for ways to make the person you made special in your life want more out of the relationship but they are full of games. The most attractive thing about someone should be their level of commitment, faithfulness, trust and honesty.

People who are in these types of relationships, where someone does not want to give their heart freely, often find themselves in competition with others for that person's affections by using distractions through everyday life situations to take away from what needs to be talked about. No matter if you are the woman or man who is involved with a commitment phobe be prepared to be jealous because you're starving in your relationship for commitment. A person can't give you what they don't have inside to give you, let it go. If they are not willing to make those crucial changes in their life to fit you in than, you are just spinning your wheels in hopes that love bites them in the butt as it has you.

Right now you're probably feeling at a loss for words due to what's taking place in your relationship. But trust me when I tell you that the commitment phobe in your life is just full of smoke and mirrors. If you have been asking some tough questions within the last few days or weeks in your relationship, their behavior is not unusual. You need to understand that a commitment phobe does not want to be pushed in a corner with questions about commitment, especially by you.

They will never be able to give you what it is you are looking for in a relationship because they don't have it to give. Trust that if they had the qualities they claim to possess, you would see it and most of all experience it. Struggling to understand the many reasons why they are not opening up their heart is not important, you are important. The key to keeping your sanity in times like this simply has to do with seeing who and what it is you are really dealing with. What do you expect from this person you now know is a commitment phobe? What are you prepared to do if you are not given the opportunity to their heart?

As I mentioned earlier many people who are dating today including you, have experienced some form of hurt in past relationships, for this reason many people still walk around with a an emotionaly guarded heart. If you want to get past your fears of the next relationship then you must pay close attention to how fast things have changed in your relationship today. We all have the ability to learn from our mistakes if we really want too. But If you are looking for this relationship to work itself out, you will have to be real about your feelings and the person you are dating, seeing them as a commitment phobe is the first place you want to start. They know who and what they really are, it's you who is just finding out. It's not difficult to love another human being but it is difficult if they are not looking for love or are afraid to love. Stop putting yourself on the battle field for this person who is not willing to fight for you. If you still want the relationship then ask the difficult questions but be open to their answers since they may be unwilling to change their views on who and what they are for you. Also, know that you will be on a rollercoaster ride with a commitment phobe who tells you that they need time and doesn't see any value in committing to anyone.

There are many ways to detect if you are being pushed to the side by a commitment phobe who will not commit to you. Below are signs you can look for that indicate you are dealing with a blocking distraction.

- No time is the right time for your questions, they remember they have something to take care of but will get back to your question when they return. It never happens.
- It's all a joke, your feelings and emotions are criticized rather than understood. Even more so if you are a man you are looked at as soft and sensitive, for a woman she is looked at as clingy which is hurtful to both when coming from the commitment phobe who has these fears.
- Let things happen naturally is always the answer a commitment phobe likes to give, because it's the easiest way to say get off my back.
- Compare and contrast is another way your commitment phobe tends to distract away from growing the relationship, they do so by comparing you to everything past, present and future.

- o Role reversal is a safe haven the commitment phobe can hide behind by making you look too weak or overly aggressive while having you to believe that you are in a gender role reversal.
- o When I am ready is one that the commitment phobe also struggles with since it allows them to set the course of the relationship in their favor. Many relationships stop growing when the relationship is in this state. There is no clear time or moment when the commitment phobe will be real with you, it will allow him or her to play more mind games while protecting themselves from future hurt.
- o It's all in your mind is where your relationship ends up since you are not allowed to see it, nor touch it the way it should be touched to grow, because your relationship is ran by fear, not love.

I know this may not be something you want to think about but like many out here dating, you need help making your relationship work which is understandable. A lot of times we have no control in who we fall in love with, but we do have control of our actions and feelings. Sometimes loving someone with commitment issues feels like a prison but you are not locked away, there are so many things you can do to change what's going on even if that's walking away. Below are things you can do to help your relationship to grow but remember you can't force someone to treat you the way you want to be treated.

- o Question everything if you want a commitment phobe to respect you, question those things that you see in your relationship that do not make sense. The commitment phobe will not like it and try to gain control of the situation by threatening to leave the relationship or make themselves a victim once they see you refuse to be the victim of their behavior.
- o Take it as lies is the best way to deal with a commitment phobe since many will say whatever you need them to say to make you feel good about yourself. Know your own self-worth, never look for your relationship to be based on good feel words, make the commitment phobe prove themselves since that is what they want you to do.

- Don't believe everything you hear which that is how the commitment phobe gets your heart, once you fall for their every word they pull back and you are no longer worthy of them. Just as you are looking for someone to believe in you they are looking for you to believe everything they say.
- If you say so is the attitude the commitment phobe in your life loves to have with everything. They do not take flattering words well, they have to prove themselves and they do so through excuses and lies.
- Be willing to probe, in many relationships with a commitment phobe the person finds themselves accepting everything, not questioning anything even when the signs are clear. If they are keeping part of their life secret from you probe until you can't probe anymore, trust me when I say the commitment phobe will try to hide. This allows him/her to see that you are not a sucker for a good feeling and a relationship built on IOUs.
- Walk away, this one may be the hardest especially if you have put in hard work to getting the relationship going in the right direction. When you see the relationship is no longer moving forward, it's not because of you but the other person's fear to move on then you must walk away.
- Never allow your relationship to block you from growing as a person, know that a commitment phobe is more interested in the act of love rather than the feel of love. Most are actors and actresses who have very guarded hearts. Not all individuals who suffer with commitment phobias come from broken homes or may have seen something disturbing in their life. I have known many people with commitment phobias who find themselves in this place due to broken relationships and failed marriages. They are now unwilling to let anyone in even though they are still looking for love. When you learn that a commitment phobe is unable to love you because they are too busy protecting themselves from being hurt by love this is when you will understand where your relationship stands.

Realizing it is over

You finally have come to the end of your rope with this relationship, now you are ready to give it up because you're drained from trying to work it out. Really you should not be surprised by the realization that your relationship is ending since you have been on this road with a commitment phobe for some time now. Now that you are ready to walk away they are the ones fighting for the relationship to work but you have been down this road so many times that you have lost count. What have you learned? Why should you stay? These are the questions that are stuck in your mind. Can I do this again? Is it worth it? The true answer is within you, that is what you should be listening too.

A commitment phobe will wait until the relationship is so stressed out, that it flat lines before jumping back in to save it one last time, but this is to make them feel good about themselves instead of feeling like a failure. They know what you can take and what you can't take and love to see you in this mental state, most would say it's cruel seeing you this way. Not every relationship with a commitment phobe ends in days, weeks or months some last for years believe it or not and the person who wants everything to work out ends up struggling alone in the relationship. No matter how much progress you make with a commitment phobe they will always reset themselves back to what they feel is their truth which ends up with them not committing to you.

Many times a commitment phobe will not allow themselves to be burdened down by such feelings of love and commitment because they know they were never really going to stay. But they play a very strong role as if they are affected when clearly they are not. I know many people who went through this only to come to the truth that they had to move on with their lives. This happened when they realized that the loving person they were with was more like a death or cancer in their life rather than something good.

It seems easy enough when dealing with someone who has not truly experienced love, by teaching them how to love. When you are dealing with a commitment phobe love is not an option since they are fearful of it. It's like you are dealing their past they are not able to let go. You will never change that fact, you believe that you can love another person so much that they will stop hurting. That way of thinking is what keeps you holding on and being fooled. No one can love someone past their hurt and pain, it is up to that person to let go and move on. The only role you will end up playing with a commitment phobe is the one they allow you to play in their life and from where I am sitting it's more like a hit and run.

When you realize that you can't change someone's way of thinking about love and commitment, you will stop lying to yourself and allowing that person to love you too death by making you unhappy and miserable. You may be hurt now that you are giving up on the relationship or maybe you feel like you are giving up too soon but ask yourself this, aren't you tired? Why are you the only one fighting for this relationship to work? Your freedom to the life and type of relationship you want is on the other side of this relationship once you let go.

So realize that you've went through a lot in such a short period of time, all the love and emotions that you felt for this person is now filled with disgust and anger. Don't let these feelings make you become the next commitment phobe in a relationship. Forgive yourself for staying and putting up with all of the things you put up with and move on, with no regret.

Your happiness is based on your ability to forgive yourself for staying with a broken person, from that you can move on to bigger and better things. Once you let go, keep that door closed by not allowing that person to run in and out of your life, that is how you start the healing process. You should never be afraid to search for love but know that it's love you are attracting to you and nothing else. On the other side of your hurt and pain is the relationship you have been looking for. Now is the time to go to it, just make sure you leave your past hurts, anger and mixed emotions with the commitment phobe.

Many people say when things don't go your way in life, smile and move on. When you do this, you will see that you will be better off alone then stuck with someone who is holding on to life situations like that of a life jacket. In their case their life jacket doesn't work and is more like a death jacket or a death trap, they are going down fast and you were entangled in it before you broke free. Now you see yourself free falling to something so much better for you, smile you are on your way.

12 CHAPTER
KEEPING IN TOUCH

Now that you have moved on and out of the commitment phobe's life who made your life miserable they want to keep in touch. How sweet but I say cut your losses and don't look back. What could they offer you that they could not offer you in a relationship. The truth is if they could not commit to you in a relationship what type of friend could they be. The only thing a commitment phobe wants when a relationship is over is to have a chance to run in and out of your life, keep them moving. They love playing on your past emotions and the old feelings you had for them, they love to be wanted, don't do it. *Don't fall* for the I'm over you so let's keep in touch role, this old game is played out. You owe them nothing but a nice happy good bye.

Now this is where the commitment phobe will try to get you to accept that you may still have feelings for them since you are not able to be friends, no hard feelings, right. Wrong they are not looking to be your friend and you need to see this and fast. If you are trying to move on with your life and forget what happened in your last relationship then you must do so leaving them completely alone. This means no phone calls, texting, email or chatting with them on social media. I know it's a lot to ask you to do but you want to move on right? This is how you do it, you never keep negative people in your life. This person has to find their place in life just like you and they can't do it by emotionally beating up on their relationships and hurting others. I am sure you don't support that type of behavior from anyone which is one of the reason why you left them to begin with. If you want to be a good friend tell them to get help and stop hurting others.

I have had many friends and love ones fight to hold on to people like this who mean them no good. They are more attached to their hurts and pains then experiencing all that life has to offer. I have also witnessed the person with commitment issues fighting to stay in the life of the person they made miserable in an effort to sabotage any future relationships. You simply can't have your cake and eat it too without some form of backlash for taking along the wrong person. Learn to leave the past where it belongs, in the past.

If you have not asked yourself these questions now is the time. Why is my ex trying to stay in my life? Are they still playing mind games? These question hold the key to your happiness or your misery. Why should I make them a friend? Why am I considering keeping them around my life? Have I truly let them go? Why can't I move on? What if we are better off as friends? Maybe if I keep them around they will want me back? No matter what your reasoning is for keeping around your ex who did not care about your heart and feelings, you should not do it. I am all for forgive and forget but I have a hard time with people who keep around the problem that almost took their heart and kept them heartbroken.

Are you still holding on to some glimmer of hope by considering keeping this person in your life? This time you are the one playing mind games and the end will not be in your favor. This is an area better left to a commitment phobe not a trusting and loving person.

Here is the kicker, you need time to recover which means that you should not jump into the next relationship that comes along. You need time to make sure depending on how long you were in a relationship with a commitment phobe, that you have not lost your idea of love and commitment. You have to also heal your heart so that you do not hold back your feelings from someone in the future because of what was done to you. You know how that feels and no one wants to be played with so moving on with your life is the best thing you can do even if that means getting new friends and going to different places to hang out so that you don't run into that person anytime soon.

Know that it's okay to give yourself permission to be hurt, disappointed and angry since you were lied too and trusted someone who did not deserve it. Keeping a commitment phobe as a friend or someone to talk is not a good idea. If you are still in love with them they can affect your life in a negative way, let them go!

I remember the time when a good friend of mine was deeply in love with this guy who she had dated for over a year. The closer she got to him the harder he was on her, he was not happy seeing her happy without making her cry the next day. I mean this guy lived by the words I'm sorry because he was every time and it took a toll on their relationship. He did not want to let her go for fear she would find someone better and true to their feelings so he kept her in a I love you state of mind. I have to give it to her because she stayed with him as long as she could stay with him until she felt like he was driving her mad.

He picked arguments and made nasty and mean comments when there was no reason for it. He always had an out as to why it was happening which had to do with either is past life, family issues she knew nothing about since he did not like her around his family as much or something at work. It got to where she could time when he was going to say something that would ruin whatever mood they were in by the closeness they were having. Still she found it hard to believe that the man she was in love with had commitment issues because he was so sweet and confident, yet his sweetness would turn on her at a drop of a dime.

He was good with words and making her feel good whenever he was around, but he began to use that power by making her cry because his words were cruel. One minute he wanted to get close and have a good time, the next he could not take things seriously, it was like he was unplugged from his emotions. Their connection to each other would be short lived by insults or fights. This is what he subjected her to for the course of their relationship, she put up with it because dating a commitment phobe can be confusing. And it definitely was for her many times.

I remember when he walked out, she took that time to look over her life and thought that there was not enough love she could give him that would make him comfortable in loving her the way she needed to be loved. She packed up her heart and left the relationship. If you are wondering if he tried to stay in her life let me be the first to tell you, he sure did. She tried it for a week and found that he was even more cruel and angrier now that he was not in her life. He became judgmental of everyone she went out with and even tried to make her jealous by trying to date one of the women she worked with.

She had had enough and banned him from her life no texting, talking on the phone, no social media, no meeting up for drinks, he was gone and she told me it was hard but when she took control of her life and put him completely out. She felt a sense of control over her fears and emotions something she had not felt in such a long time since dating him.

This is where you need to be in your life if you are trying to get away from a damaged person whose unable to receive and give love. Is it your idea to keep them in your life as a friend or did they have some type of say about it? Remember a commitment phobe is good with words and convincing others to give in when they are not willing to give in to you.

Don't be fooled by being friends with a commitment phobe unless you are looking to be unhappy. Know that you can move on and love again no matter how hard it seems, or how scary it is. Know that you don't have to be lied too or controlled in order to have someone in your life. You are worth so much more, can't you see that. Know that you are not a victim since the only victim in this relationship was the person who is unable to love or feel love. If anything, you gave them a chance to experience something real that they did not understand.

Later on you will be glad you were able to let go and move on in your life to bigger and better things. As far as for your ex's relationships they may be stuck forever being a commitment phobe. Below are a few signs to look out for when your commitment phobe ex tries to stay in your life long after the relationship is over.

- o "Can we still text from time to time," is what the commitment phobe says when they know they have ruined the relationship. This is to show you that there are no hard feelings on their end because the relationship did not work out. Another role reversal in action, *wink, wink.*

- o "No harm in talking on the phone," is another way your ex commitment phobe lover tries to use to stay a part of your life. This is to keep watch over who you are dating next, not that they can ever commit to you, it's for their peace of mind and allows them to see if you are truly over them as you say.
- o "Let's hang", is one of the slick moves of an ex commitment phobe lover who wants benefits without commitment uses feeling that you may owe them that since you two were in a previous relationship. This is strictly a move for sexual favors. *Pretty damn, slick, I tell you.*
- o "Friends forever", is another little sneaky trick an ex commitment phobe lover will use in order to still have some form of control over your life and the things that you do. To give them this benefit after proving they are not fit for a relationship that is full of commitment is once again setting your life up for more hurt. If they could not do right by you in a committed relationship, what makes you think they can as a friend? *Child, please keep it moving.*

Many times in life I have witnessed friends of mine making things harder than what they really were by keeping around those ex-lovers who were not committed to them as friends who end up destroying their next relationship. I simply say," If you did not have a good feeling about your relationship and had to end it, then that feeling still applies to having that person anywhere in your life."

Too many times I see where treating someone better than they have treated you ends up hurting that person more than when they were in a relationship with you. You simply can't change someone because you are good, honest, committed and faithful. You have to see people for who and what they are and adjust your life according to that or you will continue to be used, hurt, broken hearted and misused by others who are not like you. *Check mate!*

Dating Again

Let me be the first to tell you that there is no easy way in getting back into the dating world sometimes you will have trust issues after being with a commitment phobe. The easiest way to start again is to trust your instinct when it tells you something is not right. Now that you are single you are getting hit on more than ever, or maybe it's the opposite and no one is looking your way but you are sure looking in their direction. This does not mean that you have the word sucker, or I have been hurt written across your forehead and others are picking up on it like a radar.

You will find yourself a little more apprehensive in your next relationship and more likely to hide your feelings in order to protect yourself from getting hurt and lied to again. Know that this is normal, but don't allow yourself to stay stuck in this mindset because it would only undermine everything you are not. It's nothing wrong with trusting others and giving them the benefit of the doubt until they prove to you that they are not worth trusting.

I've seen the effects of how one can change who they are after being involved with a commitment phobe once the relationship is over. I have also seen loving and trusting friends of mine become bitter and cold hearted in their next relationship all because of what was done to them by someone they felt they could trust.

Maybe this was your first time ending a relationship with commitment phobe, now you are not sure who you can trust or if you feel you would ever open up your heart again to someone. Don't let one bad experience, or even a few bad experiences stop you from looking for that special person who belongs in your life. If you are not really ready to get back in the dating world but you have family and friends pushing you to date again just tell them that you need time to get past your break up and that in no time you will be dating again.

In the meantime trust your instinct when something does not feel right, do not turn a blind eye because you are interested in the person and feel that you can make them fall in love with you because of how you are, that's the mindset that allows so many people to become victims of this type of relationship. In order to not make the same mistakes in your next relationship you need to ask yourself, what did you learn in your last relationship? What red flags did you notice early on in the relationship that you simply ignored? Was there any inconsistences in their behaviors? Where their clues you turned a blind eye to for the sake of making the relationship work? How often did you catch them in a lie?

These are the questions one should ask themselves when in a new relationship, this is the key in seeing the truth in the relationship working verses not working. Now that you have these questions to think about you may want to apply them to your new relationship or one you are thinking about starting. It's your job to investigate the state of any and every relationship you find yourself in no matter what you feel is going on. If you are still unclear of what signs and red flags you need to look for when dealing with a commitment phobe the below list shall make things easy for you.

o   Honesty is the key in making any relationship a success, so make sure the next person you are dating or looking to date is someone you can trust and is honest with you about their past and present relationships.

o   Trust in a relationship is another key to having a successful relationship, knowing that you can trust the person you are dating says a lot about your relationship.

o   Consistency is another major player in having a relationship that work because it leaves out the confusion of where you stand in a relationship. Not knowing from day to day the state of mind of the person you are dating can become very frustrating as well as destroy your relationship.

o   Communication is also key in making a strong relationship even stronger no matter what comes your way.

o   Respect is another key that aids in the foundation of building a strong relationship that is pleasing to both people. If your partner does not feel respected then you're not insuring and investing in the future of your relationship. Learn to be a team player!

Always remember that a strong foundation is essential for the success of any relationship, without those keys mentioned above in your next relationship, you are sure to face the same issues again. You never want to make the next person you date responsible for what happened in your last relationship. Although this is understood sometimes it's not avoided and you find yourself just a little bit harder on the next person for what you've went through in your last relationship.

Allow yourself time to get over your hurts and fears of dating again because trust me it can be scary, it seems like the next person comes along saying similar things that hooked you in your last relationship and you know how that turned out. No one expects you to jump right in a relationship after everything you just went through except for a few friends and loved ones who want to see you smiling again, but understand that's their way of helping you get over everything and moving on in your life.

You don't need to prove anything to anyone on how you are dealing with dating again. As long as you know that it's your choice in when you start dating again. Stop beating yourself up for not seeing the clues in your past relationship, learn to move on and not fault yourself because the most important thing is that you got out and did not allow it to continue. You will have a better and more successful future now that you know what a commitment phobe is.

A good rule of thumb when you start dating again, is to keep an open mind and know that just because someone tells you the same or similar things that were said to you in your previous relationship doesn't mean that you are dealing with another commitment phobe. Once you've dated a commitment phobe you will be more in tune to the ways and behaviors that are distinct and clear.

Reinventing a New You

Reinventing a new you is not hard but it's necessary after a break up. Taken all that you have been through in trying to make a relationship work with someone you thought you knew but who turned out to be a liar and a fake is a hard pill to swallow. You must know that not everyone is going to celebrate your success not even the person you thought was the best thing that had ever happen to you once you found out the true nature of their games. I know you are hurting and that smile on your face is a way to show those close to you that you are no longer affected. You suffered disgrace, hurt and lies in your relationship and smiled your way through it around those you loved.

Knowing that life is short as one would always say tells you that feeling sad and down about being lied to is not going to change the outcome of what took place, you simply have to pull it together and move on. Do you remember those days when you were the happiest in your life and it seemed like nothing else mattered? What about the days when you felt good about the direction you were moving in before getting involved with someone who sought to hurt and destroy your life with secrets and lies. You have to know that you are stronger than you know and will get past those feelings and emotions in no time. Right now I want you to act as if you are past those emotions by not allowing yourself to relive all of the bad things that took place in your life.

Can you see the sunshine ahead and smell the fresh air around you? Can you picture yourself happy in love and with the person you were meant to be with? Can you smile when everything inside of you tells you to cry? How you see through this time of transition in your life will prepare your heart for the next journey in your life and trust me when I tell you that you will not want to miss out on that journey. We all know that life is full of surprises some good and some bad especially when it comes to letting someone in your heart but it should never stop you from being who you are.

See yourself past this moment and soon you will feel your heart healing, even if this means you must let go some of the things you love having when you were in that not so happy relationship. Many times we try to take the past into the future and it just does not work out the way we want it and that's okay. Be willing to box up some good times you had in the form of pictures and gifts given to you from a past relationships that did not work out and move on. Below are a few things I recommend after your relationship is over?

- o Have fun and live life.
- o Give yourself a makeover. Nothing says it's a new day like getting a makeover.

- o Letting go of old memories is a great way to start a new life and a new you. Box up your past if you have too!
- o Think on the next person you would like to meet. What are some qualities you would like the next person you date to have?
- o Stay away from negative people who only seek to remind you of how messed up your relationship really was.
- o Travel somewhere you have never been before and take a friend or someone you trust that will keep you laughing.
- o Know that you are worth love and that you will find it when you are ready.
- o Decorate your place and get out of the past by adding a splash of color or scented candles that put you in a relaxed mood.

There are still so many things that you can do to help move past your hurt and start a new life but it will have to take you wanting to move forward. Worrying about the things that made you unhappy when you felt that you were in a good place will only keep you down. Life is what you make it and not everyone in life has a great relationship story to tell but know that your story is for your growth to a better you.

Give yourself credit for getting out of a bad situation we all know was not easy but guess what, you did it. You are the key to your own happiness and that happiness starts with you.

Stay Away from Takers

I am sure about now you have a clear understanding of what a commitment phobe is after all of the chapters you have read but don't be fooled into thinking that you have nothing to worry about as you move forward in dating and meeting new people. You still must carry a bit of caution when making friends or dating, this is the rule. Although your heart and intentions may be good not everyone else's is and for this reason you have to look at everyone as a suspect until you have a clear understanding of who and what you are dealing with.

Let's say for instance you have just gotten out of a bad relationship and know that the person you were dating before was a commitment phobe you ignored the red flags and warning signs for the sake of giving someone a chance but it did not work. I am sure you had that gut feeling that something was not right with this person or they were just too good to be true. Let's say that you dating them anyway and you are happy to be out of that worthless relationship. I am sure you have a million negative things you can say to justify your feelings and emotions but you must know that those feelings and emotions will not keep you from the next commitment phobe who will enter your life.

These folks are takers, a taker will never give you what you want unless you move clearly away from them, they will only follow you because they are looking for something like you are looking for something, for them it's to lie to your face.

That old give and take is not always and for a commitment phobe take is all they know how to do which is why they leave their victims in a relationship devastated. To insure that your next relationship is one that is healthy and safe you have to put the nice person aside when you see red flags popping up all around you. Nice people never get the person or the relationship that they really want because they are too busy being used as a doormat.

Letting someone wipe their feet on your heart is never okay and should never be accepted as a way of getting to know someone or worse keeping someone in your life. I am sure you are probably thinking, who would allow someone to do that to them, but you would be surprised what people would do to have someone in their life.

Someone with commitment phobias are focused and know what they want and what they will not allow which means they are selfish while you are trusting. Last time I checked those I love in relationships, even friendships like this were left heartbroken. If you are that person that feels you can get anyone to love you because you have that effect on others you need to really think again when dealing with people who have these issues. The more problems a person has the more it will reflect in their inability to have a successful and long lasting relationship with anyone.

We all have been around someone in our life who wants more, needs more and asks for more than they are willing to give. We see them in their everyday life and swear to ourselves that we will never date or marry such a person because we have witnessed this behavior around us still we find ourselves in relationships like this years later. Are you asking yourself how in the heck did you get here? Why have you accepted a person who does not respect you? Why are you settling for someone who swore they will never marry you? Why are you so afraid of being alone? What is it about this person that makes you disregard everything you told yourself you would never accept or tolerate? Why are you allowing yourself to be used?

Are you willing to walk in this relationship with your eyes closed? Are you closing your eyes when the red flags pop up so that you don't have to deal with it or better yet make a decision? These are important questions that you should be asking yourself now that you've found yourself another commitment phobe and is thinking about dating someone that may not be stable in terms of what they are looking for in a relationship. First you have to know the signs of a taker since most people who date commitment phobes tend to draw the same type of person around them every time.

- o A taker is someone that wants you to prove yourself to them, but sits in judgment of you.
- o A taker is someone who is always right and never wants to compromise especially if it will make them wrong.
- o A taker is someone who tells you what they want and doesn't care how you feel.
- o Takers never play by the rules of dating because they have been used, hurt and suffer with low self-esteem, they are only looking for a pick me up through hurting others like yourself.
- o A taker does not care about your heart or if they break it, they are more concerned about not getting hurt by anyone so their mindset is, I will get you before you get me.
- o A taker is an enemy to the relationship and love.
- o A taker wants to prove that they are right with how they treat people because of all the wrong they have encountered.

o A taker sees you as a prize in a game and the game is how fast they can convince you to believe them.
o A taker sees relationships through your eyes, yet carries a destructive mentality in order to feel safe whenever they are with you.

If you are dating for looks you are one step closer to finding a commitment phobe. I try to tell others to weigh out the person's heart and don't just take their word for it. I am sure we all have that relationship resume that paints us in a good light when we may be far from that and have a lot of work ahead of us on how we see relationships. The world around us is one that is built on taking, therefore you will see more takers than givers. Now this does not mean that you will never find the person that you want, it just means that you will have to be a little more patient and understanding when you are dating. You also have to not be taken by smooth words and nice outings during dating because many people get caught up in the dating process and forget about the person they are truly dating.

Focus is the key to dating, not nice words, complements or how much money someone is willing to spend on you since in the end it will mean nothing if the person has a takers mindset. This is the same behavior of a commitment phobe whether they are male or female, they have to put in a little investing to get a quick return on those investments that they put or ends up being heartfelt emotions that are believable. The quick return is your open, trusting heart that they are looking to take along with sex, money and whatever they feel they can get from you now that you are open to them.

Have you ever been around someone that is in love literally overnight, but you are trying to get them to see things clearly so that they won't get hurt but they see you as a hater to their new relationship. After a few weeks or months their relationship has fizzled down to nothing and they are looking for love again more trusting than they were before. If you have seen this happen to someone you know then you witnessed the return of the commitment phobe.

For young women out there who are allowing themselves to get pregnant for a man simply because he said he is ready for a family, but not marriage this should be a red flag, that you are dealing with a commitment phobe. Who on earth will want the responsibility of a child but not as a full time parent? If you are allowing yourself to get pregnant for the sake of keeping your relationship intact, for the sake of someone who at the drop of a hat wants something, than you are allowing yourself to be victimized by a commitment phobe.

Do you feel a child should have the support of both parents? Do you feel that a child should see both of their parents? This is not addressing those relationships who have tried to make it work and realize that it's over. These questions are for those young and some old foolish loves who are requesting things in a dating phase with no chances of having a full committed relationship. Maybe you have asked the question of commitment and marriage and received a yes, maybe you have asked those questions and received mixed answers. This is when you should be receiving that gut feeling telling you what's really going on.

I know that gut feeling is not one of popular conversations because it's a big indicator that something is wrong, something you don't want to have to face or deal with. Still we are all built with this indicator inside of us whether we use it or not.

If you know you are dating someone who is not good for you and they have sent you mixed messages in the name of love, it's time to get out of that relationship. The longer you stay with someone who is not willing to give you what you need the more you lose bits and pieces of who you are and the more you die inside. The worse part of all of this is that you leave the relationship as a commitment phobe and hurt someone else.

- o Stop the cycle of killing those who love you because of bad choices you've made in your past.
- o Stop the cycle of dating people who are not fit to be in your life.
- o Stop the cycle of giving people a chance because you believe in love.
- o Stop the cycle of giving everyone the benefit of the doubt.
- o Stop the cycle of killing and ruining your life because you don't want to be alone.

o   Stop the cycle of lying to yourself.
o   Stop the cycle of ignoring that gut feeling that's trying to keep you safe.
o   Stop the cycle of having a broken heart.
o   Stop the cycle of going back to a commitment phobe.
o   Stop the cycle of dating your exes, they are your exes for a reason.
o   Stop the cycle of allowing people to lie to your face.
o   Stop the cycle of thinking you can change how people think.
o   Stop the cycle of pretending you don't see what's going on.

Just stop it! If you love yourself, your job is to protect your heart and you can do that by not allowing yourself to tricked, fooled and lied too. Where ever you are in your life today look at it as a time for growth and only allow those people in your life who are capable of growing with you.

o   Trust yourself.
o   Love yourself.
o   Be kind to yourself.
o   Know that you deserve the best.
o   Protect your heart from strangers.
o   Learn to listen without trusting or giving away your heart.
o   Keep your emotions in control.
o   Don't make sex your reason for love, know that attraction can be seen in the heart and physical attraction can be a distraction from ones heart if that's all you look for.

Follow your heart when it comes to what's right and wrong trust your gut feeling even if that person is telling you to trust them. No one knows you like you know yourself and that's what you have in your corner. How many times did you feel like something was wrong and you were right? How many times have you seen through someone knowing they were no damn good for you and was proven right later on? So, why on earth are you not trusting yourself?

If you want something good, you will know it when it comes, if you just want something quick you are opening up yourself and your heart, to death. Love is not death but commitment phobes are, so as long as you have those two in your rear view mirror, you are bound to steer clear from a head on collision with your heart.

Never be that person who tells themselves, I told you so! So the next time you see signs of a commitment phobe heading your way, run away yelling no thank you!

39491341R00073

Made in the USA
Lexington, KY
25 February 2015